Bolton

Corporation Transport

Harry Postlethwaite

with additional research by
Derek Shepherd

© 2007 Venture Publications Ltd

ISBN13 978 1905 304 165

Contents

Front cover illustration: The striking appearance of the full-fronted PD2s delivered in 1962, and sporting the new cherry red and white livery, is seen to good advantage of UBN 903, No. 170, when new. *(STA)*

Rear cover illustration: A splendid panorama with one of Bolton's distinctive Atlanteans set amongst the town centre archticture and showing a good selection of contemporary cars. *(STA)*

Introduction

Historically, the town of Bolton was very much at the centre of the extensive Lancashire cotton industry and prior to local Government reorganisation in 1974, when it became part of Greater Manchester, it was the largest town in Lancashire. It also had the largest municipal transport fleet apart from the cities of Liverpool, Manchester and Salford. Another claim to fame was that it was the home town of the late Fred Dibnah who entertained many in his inimitable way with his demolition of chimneys, many of them associated with the Lancashire cotton industry, and also with his fascination of the subject of steam which led to a wonderful television series screened by the BBC in 2006, after Fred's death.

The 1897 Municipal Handbook described the County Borough of Bolton as 'thoroughly businesslike with their capacity of organising commercial enterprises unsurpassed'. Bolton became a Borough in 1838, and then achieved County Borough status in 1888 when it was also awarded an official coat of arms.

When the Corporation purchased the lease and rolling stock from the former horse tram operator in 1899 it became one of the early municipal operators in the north west, two years ahead of both Manchester and Salford. It had already built its own electricity generating station, at Spa Road, and was thus in a good position to undertake the operation of electric trams, unlike Manchester, again as an example, where the tramway opening was delayed until sufficient power was available.

The author's first recollection of Bolton Transport goes back to childhood in Whitehaven during World War 2 and the sight of Bolton Transport No. 21 operating on hire to Cumberland Motor Services; this and other reminiscences including hirings will appear later in the story.

Bolton's transport department, like many others, operated efficiently – and made a very substantial contribution to the local rates – until 1969 when, to the dismay of virtually all concerned, the undertaking lost its identity when it became part of the then-new but now long-forgotten SELNEC organisation. This and much more will become clear as this brief history takes us through the life-and-times of one of the north west's most interesting operators.

A map from a Bolton Town Guidebook dating from 1930 and clearly showing the strength of manufacturing and the importance of the ports in north west England. Bolton, naturally, was seen to be at the very heart of the region. *(DS collection)*

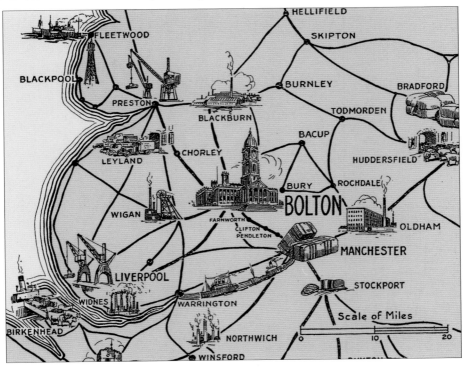

Tramway Development

In 1878 Bolton Council, in partnership with the neighbouring councils of Farnworth and Astley Bridge, obtained powers to construct 17 miles of horse tramway which was then leased, by a series of 21 year leases, to E Holden and Company, who were operators of horse bus services in the area. The rent was set at five and three eighths percent of the cost of construction and equipment, including rolling stock, giving a figure which in 1896 amounted to £3,801.10s.5d per annum over 21 years. The operation of trams commenced on 1st September 1880 with services from Bolton to Moses Gate, Bolton to Halliwell and Bolton to Dunscar. In 1888 the three councils obtained powers to operate the tramways mechanically. Steam tram engines were favoured, being already used on other local tramway systems, but cable haulage was also considered. The Fireless Motor Syndicate of Manchester proposed the introduction of cars powered by ammonia gas, and trial trips were actually made, but, perhaps thankfully, it came to naught and the horse drawn trams continued.

The fleet included examples of the Eades Patent design whereby the single-ended cars were rotated on a special turntable under the body, allowing them to turn round at the terminus, but avoiding the need to detach the horses, and, in the case of double-deck cars, greatly reducing the weight of the body by doing away with one staircase. These trams were manufactured by the Manchester Carriage Company at its Pendleton, Salford, works, under the direction of the designer and patentee John Eades and his son, also called John, but were assembled in Bolton by Holden's. Double-deck cars were drawn by three horses and single-deck by two horses.

A map showing the extent of the horse tram network operated by Edmund Holden and Company between 1880 and 1899, with termini located several miles out of the town centre to the north, south and west. Forty-eight horse trams operated over the system's 18 track miles. *(66 Group)*

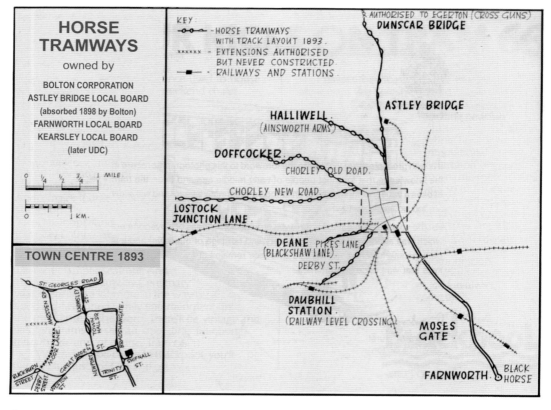

A good load on one of Holden's knifeboard-seated horse buses, above, with this one bound for Horwich. The view below shows a familiar sight in days when horses were widely used for public and private transport – the stone water troughs which provided drinking water for the animals. This one stood at the junction of what is now the A666 Bolton-Blackburn road, where the Dunscar tram can be seen, with the road going over the moors through Belmont to Preston to the right and out of view. The A58 ring road now crosses at this point. *(66 Group)*

The Bolton Extension Act 1897 brought about the absorption of Astley Bridge Urban District Council and Bolton Rural District Council which meant that the Astley Bridge tramway became the property of Bolton Corporation. By 1897 Holden's lease on the tramway was approaching its end and Bolton sought and obtained powers to operate the tramway extending it into adjacent council areas and to Horwich.

Horwich was home to the giant Lancashire & Yorkshire railway company's workshops which at that time employed some 3,000 on the manufacture and repair of its locomotives and rolling stock.

Anticipating that it would soon be operating electric tramcars in the Borough, the Corporation had constructed an electricity generating station, in Spa Road, in 1894. Now, in 1899, with matters imminent, it was able to extend the capacity of Spa Road by installing two 1,000hp and two 500hp generating sets, comprising a steam engine built by Musgrave & Son of Bolton and a dynamo from Mather & Platt of Manchester. This extra capacity was specifically for the tramways.

Nearby, over at Radcliffe, the newly-formed Lancashire Electric Power Company, one of the largest in the country, was gearing up to supply current to an area of some 1,100 square miles, from south of the river Ribble to Manchester. Down the road at Howe Bridge, Atherton, the South Lancashire Electric Transport & Power Company was also busy. It had intended to build its new generating station in Leigh but since Leigh Corporation were not being cooperative in other matters it built at Howe Bridge instead, depriving Leigh of the rateable income on the complex. The current would supply local mills, and, naturally, the SLT tram system. It generated 7,500 volts in an unusual two-phase output, rather than the usual three-phase arrangement.

All this frenzied activity stemmed from the discovery of the means of generating and distributing high voltage alternating current by a 23 year old electrical genius named Ferranti, in 1887. His Deptford, London, power station was the first in the world to have this capability. When he moved to Manchester the north west began to benefit from his abilities, and he equipped the Atherton power station; his company had a substantial shareholding in the SLT company.

In June 1899 Bolton took over Holden's stock of 48 tramcars and 350 horses and acquired the remainder of Holden's lease, which had been due to expire in 1903, for the sum of £55,000. Holden continued to operate the system under contract for six months while the Corporation set to work relaying and electrifying the system. As work progressed it was considered – wrongly as it later turned out – that most of the track was satisfactory and did not require relaying. The first depot for the new Corporation system was on the site of the former horse car shed in Shifnall Street and a small two-road shed was opened at Tonge Moor in December 1899, in time for the start of operation; just a few weeks later, in May 1900, Daubhill depot was opened.

After months of work on the conversion ready for the new form of traction, on 8th December 1899 the Board of Trade Inspector approved the

In the view of Deansgate on the facing page three horse trams can be seen, the middle one being a single-decker. Market Street crosses from left to right in front of the tram. The dark smudge in the background sky is St George's Church, hardly visible even on a bright sunny day. Above we see Market Street, Farnworth, looking more like Market Street, Manchester with so many trams, with flags and bunting out to celebrate Queen Victoria's Jubilee in 1897. Lipton's Tea and Lifebuoy soap are still familiar names today. In another three year's time electric trams would operate along here, initially hired in from Bolton until, in 1902, Farnworth acquired its own cars. Farnworth Black Horse was a familiar destination throughout the region with LUT buses terminating there until the end of their existence. In the lower picture the Gatehouse is now better known as Eagley Way, constructed after the Second War to allow access for buses going down the valley. *(66 Group)*

Bolton car 26 on the L&Y railway bridge at Moses Gate is on hire to Farnworth, mentioned earlier on page 7. Note the paper sticker for the destination. Electric trams first reached here on 2nd January 1900, but when Farnworth began its own operation Bolton's trams terminated here. *(66 Group)*

lines and on 9th December the first electrified routes to Tonge Moor, Great Lever, and Breightmet were opened. Never served by horse cars, these completely new routes were quite soon lettered 'T', 'G' and 'B'. On New Year's Day 1900 the operation of horse trams ceased and on 2nd January 1900 electric traction came into operation on routes to Halliwell, Dunscar, Moses Gate, Daubhill, Deane, Doffcocker and Lostock.

A total of 70 tramcars had been ordered for this expansion, but only 30 were delivered by the start date and initially a skeleton service was operated. This shortfall may have been due to Bolton having had second thoughts about the ability of a fleet of 70 four-wheel trams being able to cope with the potential traffic. Of the first order for those 70 cars, only numbers 8-20 were delivered to the original specification, with 6-window bodies. Cars 1-7 and 21-40 were built to the new 'Preston' standard 3-window short canopy style bodies. Numbers 60-81, arrived in 1901 as open-topped bogies with sliding vestibule screens, and 76 seats instead of the 51 seats of the four-wheelers. The missing numbers are explained as the story unfolds.

This was an extremely busy time for all builders,

with major operators placing substantial orders – often for fleets of 100 or more cars required for the start of operation – but things would change very quickly, and only a few years later the boom time had gone and several manufacturers would have gone bust.

The British Electric Car Company of Trafford Park, Manchester, was one such, but far-and-away the most spectacular collapse was that of the old-established company GF Milnes of Birkenhead. Completely mis-reading the situation, its Directors created a substantially expanded potential when they purchased land and relocated at Hadley in Shropshire, adjacent to railway and canal for ease of transport and materials, and with every modern facility. What they lacked, however, was orders and by 1904 they had gone out of business. Ultimately, the remaining major manufacturers clubbed together to purchase the facility and keep it closed, thus protecting their own businesses and interests, and keeping prices firm. By now most operators, and certainly the larger ones, had taken delivery of the large initial fleets of cars they needed, and many were now making arrangements to build their future requirements in-house.

None of this helped Bolton, unfortunately, and the large fleet of open-topped maroon and cream four-wheel and bogie cars ordered from the Electric Railway & Tramway Company of Strand Road, Preston were just some of many that were not ready when needed by their customers.

OPENING DATES – ELECTRIC TRAMS

Tonge Moor	9th December 1899
Toothill Bridge	9th December 1899
Great Lever	9th December 1899

All the horse tram routes were converted to electric working   2nd January 1900

Hulton Lane (St Helen's Rd)	May 1900
Horwich (Crown Hotel, including Lee Lane and Victoria Road)	19th May 1900
Deane (Hulton Lane)	21st December 1900
Four Lane Ends	19th July 1902
Breightmet	18th March 1905
Darcy Lever	6th May 1910
Brownlow Fold	4th May 1911
Montserrat	8th June 1923
Swan Lane	26th October 1923
Church Road	11th April 1924
Westhoughton	19th December 1924

In addition Bolton operated:-

Moses Gate – Black Horse   13th April 1900
   to 1st June 1902 (on behalf of Farnworth UDC)
Moses Gate – Clifton   13th June 1909
   to 13th December 1915
Moses Gate – Black Horse   1st May 1927
   to 12th November 1944
Moses Gate – Walkden on behalf of the
   South Lancashire Tramways Company

The first 70 trams ordered were of the 6-window type shown above, with No. 13. Only Nos. 8-20 were actually of this type, the balance being to the new 'Preston' standard with only three windows, as seen below. It has been suggested that the makers may have been caught out by Bolton's decision not to relay its horse tracks, thus needing the cars earlier than the builders might have expected. *(66 Group both)*

On the facing page we see the former horse tram track which caused Dick, Kerr to comment unfavourably (see text below). Little wonder the electric trams were suffering when running over it. This is the junction of Deansgate (crossing), with the photographer standing in Oxford Street looking up Knowsley Street. (Bolton Libraries)

The Dick, Kerr Company helped out by loaning four brand new cars from an order for nearby Stockport Corporation (which was not then ready to use them) and these were quickly put into service. They were of the Dick, Kerr Company's reversed stair layout, with canopies extended over the driver, and as such seated six extra passengers when compared to the earlier Dick, Kerr cars supplied to Bolton. They carried numbers 41-44 and were painted in full Bolton livery, being subsequently replaced by four of a batch of eight, numbered 41-48, delivered to Bolton from the Electric Railway & Tramway Co, but incorporating the Dick, Kerr layout. The Stockport cars were then repainted, again, and delivered to their intended owner. Subsequent Bolton cars were of this layout.

Car No. 49 had been on display at the 1901 Tramway & Light Railway Exhibition in London, and arrived in Bolton carrying the green and cream livery in which it had appeared there. Later in its life with Bolton it was decorated and illuminated to celebrate the Coronation in 1911, and then again to mark the Royal Visit to Bolton in 1913.

Dick, Kerr may have been called to look at the state of Bolton's track in connection with the Stockport loan, or it may have been shortly afterwards that they were obliged to report on its condition to the Corporation in less than glowing terms. Their report stated that *"Your trouble with the Bolton system is entirely due to the condition of the permanent way in the central part of the town, and in this connection we are safe in stating that the Bolton Tramways are the only case either in England or America where an attempt has been made to utilize for electric traction purposes a track used for twenty years for horse traction"*. The Borough Surveyor's reply seems to have been lost in the mists of time but suffice to say that those tracks had to be relaid.

This was only a temporary blip, however, and development of the system continued so that on 13th April 1900 the Moses Gate route was extended to Farnworth Black Horse, the Lostock route was extended to Horwich and the Deane route was extended to Hulton Lane. A further extension took place on 19th May 1900 when the short-lived Lee Lane section in Horwich was opened on the same day that Horwich depot was also opened. The Deane route was extended to Chip Hill Road on 21st December 1900.

Additional cars were now needed and in 1901 a batch of new but unused bogie double-deckers came onto the second-hand market, presumably surplus to requirements when the St Helens Corporation acquired what became the New St Helens & District system before leasing it back. These distinctive ten cars, built by Brush of Loughborough, and numbered in Bolton's fleet as 50-59, incorporated Mozeley screens, (designed by the Burnley Manager of the same name) though not the long platforms and forward facing staircases of other New St Helens cars with Mozeley fitment. The Mozeley screen protected the driver from the frontal elements, but at the price of causing howling gales to blow up the staircase to the open top deck. Many drivers were said to prefer the open platform.

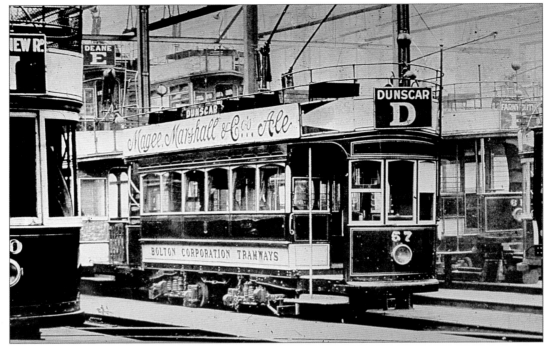

In 1900 the car shops and stables in Shiffnall Street, which had been opened in September 1880, were demolished and replaced by a new car shed and works. It was unusual when rebuilt in consisting of two back-to-back sheds, each with eight roads, but on considerably different levels – 9ft 6ins of vertical separation. Access was from Shiffnall Street or Breightmet Street, with a line running round Salop Street providing a link between the two levels. The works were adjacent to the Shiffnall Street shed, and in 1913 a completely new works would be opened extending the complex to Carlton Street. Some four years previously the original Tonge Moor depot had been closed, and converted to a cinema following the opening of Bridgeman Street depot in that same year. Bridgeman Street would be extended by an additional two roads as the system continued to expand.

On the management side, Arthur Ellis had been the Borough Electrical Engineer but in 1899 was appointed as the Corporation's first Electrical Engineer and Tramways Manager, a position which he held until June 1900 when he moved on to Cardiff Corporation as Electrical Engineer, later becoming City Electrical Engineer and Tramways Manager. His Traffic Manager at Bolton was Harry England, who had a short reign, moving on to Sunderland Corporation Transport

A depot view of one of the cars built for the New St Helens & District Tramway but never operated by that undertaking, and possibly never even delivered to them. Unused but second-hand, built by the Brush company in Loughborough, they were purchased by Bolton in 1901 from the SLT company for £701 each and numbered 50-59. *(66 Group)*

as General Manager in 1901. A local man, with two sons, Mr England was then to move to the West Riding Tramways, later West Riding Automobile Company, and became a Director of that company. He was also acting as a transport consultant, and this desire to handle 'outside' commissions may perhaps explain his short stay in Sunderland. Certainly he was a respected engineer and manager at West Riding, being frequently called to give evidence in transport enquiries, and he established links with the South Lancashire Tramways Company. He was later to become a Director of Lancashire United in 1923.

Mr England was succeeded as GM in Bolton by CC Howard, previously Assistant Manager with Liverpool Corporation Transport, and he too had a short reign, moving on in 1903. These early years were a time of flux in the industry as men were able to move to improve their positions thanks to the ever-increasing number of new tramways that were being opened. Young men seeking a promising career with long-term prospects were also attracted to the industry and some of them would become household names later in their careers.

Responding to the movement of labour, the Corporation was advertising for a new Chief Inspector, and an Assistant, in 1903. The new incumbent, Frank Armstrong, lasted less than two years before moving to Walthamstow UDC tramways as their Traffic Superintendent. *Tramway & Railway World*, reporting the move, remarked that the salary of £150 (per year!) was totally inadequate, but was pleased to see that it would be reviewed three months after the system opened. They had a point, for John Barnard, who was working his way up the ladder at Bolton, was paid £160 when he was appointed as **Assistant** Traffic Manager there in 1905.

The Tramways Committee and the Manager were busy that year, fending off another demand for half-penny fares, but also trying to keep good staff from moving away. During the autumn Assistant Engineer Frederick Taylor, having only arrived from Manchester the previous July when selected from 224 applicants for the Bolton post, was recorded as having been awarded a £50 per annum increase; the reason became clear when

it was noted that in November 1905 he was on the short list for the Manager's position at South Shields. The increase was apparently sufficient to keep him in Bolton!

Whilst salaries depended on the size of the system, the municipalities also had to contend with local Councillors who were still coming to terms – or not – with the fact the tramways department was probably going to be one of the biggest employers in the town, and that its budget and requirements for skilled administration would probably exceed the whole of the rest of any town council's labour force put together. A further complication in these early years was the jockeying for position between the Borough Electricians, the Borough Engineers, and the established former horse tramway management.

In 1905 neighbouring authority Blackburn appointed a new Chief Engineer when Leonard Johnston, who had been with the undertaking for around two years, took the Manager's post

Car number 2 of the original 1899 batch, decorated to celebrate the opening of the new route to Brownlow Fold on 4th May 1911. Alderman Miles had driven the car a short distance to mark the event. *(66 Group)*

at Gloucester. He was just 29 and had been with the British Thomson-Houston company since graduating from Finsbury College, London.

In less than ten years he had overseen on behalf of BT-H all the electrical installation at Croydon, then moving as the work was completed first to Bolton and then to Sheffield before returning to BT-H main works. He next went to BET, becoming Rolling Stock Engineer before moving to Blackburn. These were indeed times of great opportunity for the rising stars of the industry.

To give an idea of the typical salaries being paid in 1905, Leeds was paying its Tramways Superintendent £250; Blackburn and Brighton's Managers were paid £260 and £300 respectively, whilst Cheltenham's Borough Electrical Engineer was being paid £400 – electricity was still a force to be reckoned with. Putting the money into perspective, an open-top four wheeled tramcar, ready to run with all appurtenances and what would be considered a lavish and superbly-executed 'exhibition finish' by today's standards, but was then the norm even for mundane everyday public transport, cost around £500.

Arthur Albert Day was the next Tramways Manager, being appointed in 1903 and having earlier been employed by Manchester Corporation Electricity Department. He remained in post until 1913 when he retired due to ill health. The next Manager broke the mould; he was not from an electrical background and was to remain in post for a much longer period than any of his predecessors. This was the previously-mentioned John Henry Owen Barnard who had joined the Bolton staff in 1900 as a clerk, becoming Traffic Manager in 1912 and Tramways Manager in 1913. He remained in office until his death in 1938, details of which we pick up in due course.

In later years when more powerful cars with 100hp motors were put in service, the electricity department had cause to bemoan the fact that no one had warned them that such cars were coming, or of their appetite for power. Sometimes communication can be seriously impaired when changes in tradition are ignored.

We are moving ahead of our story, however. Horse trams were still being operated in other parts of Lancashire and on 2nd April 1900 a batch of 17 redundant horse trams was sold to Blackpool, St Annes and Lytham Tramways for £500. In May of the same year, Southport and

One of Farnworth's bogie cars seen on test before entering service and crossing the Long Causeway junction illustrated on page 16. These cars were destined to have an interesting life, passing to South Lancashire Transport when Farnworth ceased to be an operator, and some then passing to Bolton when SLT ceased tramway operation in 1934. They lasted in service in Bolton until the end of 1946. *(STA)*

Birkdale Tramways purchased four trams from Bolton at a cost of £23 each. The Reverend HS Patterson was one who bought a tram for £5 in 1901; strongly made from first class timber they made excellent summerhouses and sheds lasting for many decades in their new locations.

Soon after the start, route letters were used, with the letter generally being the initial letter of the outer terminus. This is claimed to have been the first instance of such route identification in the North West (ie other than the display of termini and intermediate points). Relaying and doubling of the tracks took place in 1901 and further new trams arrived together with another batch in 1903 as detailed in the Fleet Summary.

Also in 1901 fare stages were introduced, along with workmen's weekly tickets.

The Moses Gate to Black Horse route, which had been operated by Bolton on tracks owned by Farnworth UDC, was electrified from 13th April 1900. Farnworth extended the route to the boundary with Kearsley who in turn extended it to the boundary with Clifton in January 1902. Farnworth then leased the Kearsley line for 25 years, built a depot in Albert Road and bought eight open-top bogie cars with Milnes bodies, and on 1st June 1902 took over the section previously operated by Bolton who ceased to operate beyond Moses Gate. As traffic built up Farnworth found itself short of trams and as Bolton's immediate problems had now been resolved four Bolton cars were hired to Farnworth for a short period.

Farnworth's No. 13, like many others at the time, was delivered by rail to a convenient off-loading point – in this case Bolton's Trinity Street we believe. If so the single-deck horse car body in the background would be the one located there for use as a cabman's shelter – there were others around the town. *(66 Group)*

The missing panelling and other body components would be carefully packed in the lower saloon, and on the top deck, to reduce the height for transport and would then be fitted at the depot, either by representatives of the makers or by Farnworth UDC staff, before the body was united with its bogies as shown below. *(66 Group)*

The junction of Long Causeway and Albert Road in Farnworth was a major piece of trackwork and, although not symmetrical, only one pair of tracks short of a grand union. Note the jim crow attached to the left hand curve in the upper picture – this was the implement used for manual bending of the rail to create curves or to modify and correct the geometry and gauge. Scenes like this would be familiar in towns throughout the country at this time. *(66 Group)*

When Farnworth's first tram reached Walkden on 22nd June 1905 the local photographer was waiting to record the scene. Postcards would quickly be produced and on sale in his local shop, and, many years later, enthusiasts and historians would be glad of the record of the event. The man in the cap and raincoat on the rear staircase is almost certainly 'Ned' Edwardes, SLT's Power Station Engineer and later Managing Director. *(66 Group)*

The spread of manufacturing companies has been touched on already. In the early years of the 20th Century it would have been possible to buy complete tramcars from Manchester or Preston; components for those trams from most big Lancashire towns; road surfacing materials and equipment in Bolton; overhead wire, electrical equipment, batteries and so on from Chloride's factory at Clifton Junction, from St Helens or Helsby; rail and special trackwork would come from Sheffield – the list was endless. How very different from today. *(STA)*

A programme of road widening was also undertaken in 1902, increasing the width to at least 60ft on all main roads used by the tramways, and the level of activity laying tramtracks in the streets around Bolton continued undiminished, for Farnworth and South Lancashire Tramways were about to begin operation and the former's lines from Four Lane Ends were under construction.

Whereas Bolton seems to have used mainly British – and often local – companies for the construction of its tramway, the situation at Atherton was very cosmopolitan; the power station's engines came from Germany, the electrical equipment from France, rails from Belgium and the project was under the supervision of an Italian. Perhaps the SLT directors had had a bad experience with the Americans at some time, for it would have been normal for the giant American companies to be involved if British manufacturers could not supply the goods.

Since the nearby British Insulated Helsby Cables Ltd (later BICC) had connections at SLT Board level, it was no surprise that it supplied the overhead wiring. SLT began operating its trams on 20th October 1902.

In that same year a snow broom and a water sprinkler car were added to the Bolton tramway fleet, both being examples of largely forgotten maintenance vehicles needed in days when heavy winter snows could close even main roads for days or weeks on end, and hot summers could create huge amounts of dust from the unmade roads which would fill the tramway track's grooved rail and cause 'grounding' when the flow of current was impeded. (Students of these and other associated matters may be interested to know that examples of similar vehicles can be seen in the Tramway Museum at Crich, Derbyshire.)

Bolton made the news in tramway circles when in 1903 it introduced its first top-covered car, number 46, with a short enclosed 'cabin' and long open balconies. It is thought that these cars were designed in this fashion with the possibility of a covered car being blown over by strong winds being considered.

Bolton was commendably early in fitting top covers to its trams, thus protecting some of its passengers from some of the weather! Designed by Bolton's engineer Arthur Day as early as 1903, and fitted to car 46 as seen here, this design was adopted – with only minor modifications – for the rest of the Bolton fleet. Note the very short enclosed upper-deck saloon referred to in the text and the full-drop windows which made Bolton's trams distinctive and easily recognisable. The driver's rearward vision can be seen to be severely restricted by the reversed staircases. *(66 Group)*

A distinctive feature of the Bolton top cover was the lack of opening lights above the windows; all windows were full height and were designed to drop down into the upper-deck panels. This feature was retained on all Bolton-built bodies as trams were converted from open-top to enclosed configuration and the preserved example, number 66, illustrates the point perfectly.

Also in 1903, at the end of March in what at that time must have been somewhat of a marathon journey, a tram was driven in less than 4 hours from Liverpool Pier Head to Bolton Town Hall using five separate tramway systems. They travelled by way of Knotty Ash, Prescot, St Helens, Haydock, Hindley and Atherton, with – doubtless – suitable refreshment stops at each change of system. A few years later one John A Senior, grandfather of your picture researcher, apparently took his son Arthur on a tram ride from Liverpool to Patricroft which took nearly seven hours. They had travelled to Liverpool by train, one way by tram was sufficient! They were probably not interested that in Bolton workman's return fares and a parcels delivery service were also introduced in that year, though both used the Salford trams on a daily basis.

Towards the end of that year Bolton entered into contracts with the publishers of *The Manchester Evening News*, and *The Manchester*

Evening Mail, in addition to Clegg & Jones and Tillotson, both proprietors of Bolton Newspapers, for the carriage of newspapers. This led to the newspapers and newsagents giving an annual dinner for the tramwaymen in appreciation of the excellent service provided. The conveying of newspapers on trams continued for 45 years.

Above we see one of Tillotson's men unloading the evening papers from his lorry onto the front platform of a Doffcocker-bound tram – the driver will deliver them to the newsagents in the time-honoured manner by throwing the bundle into the shop doorway – if his aim is good he probably won't even stop. *(NWFA)*

The first cars to join the fleet complete with top covers – numbers 82-85 – came from Dick, Kerr's factory in 1903, but although the short top-deck saloon was retained, the window arrangement was very different. The Bolton design would become the standard, as already mentioned. *(66 Group)*

There always seemed to be children around when the photographer set up his tripod; here we see the Dunscar Bridge terminus c1903 with car 63. In 1901 the original LUT company had proposed building the Bolton, Turton and Darwen Light Railway which, at 9½ miles long, would have linked Dunscar to Darwen Corporation's Whitehall terminus, with a branch to Belmont. It came to naught. *(66 Group)*

Motor Buses – A Brief Encounter

In 1904 Bolton became the first motor bus operator in the area, using a Stirling single-deck omnibus with an enormous radiator, on a route from Brownlow Fold to Darcy Lever from 5th to 20th September when the experiment was terminated. The bus was replaced by horse drawn waggonettes of which one contemporary report stated that they 'were at least reliable'.

Nearby Lancashire United Tramways had also been experimenting with Scott-Stirling motorbuses, with equally unsatisfactory results. Their vehicles, which had been assembled in London, were second-hand from the London Power Omnibus Company, newly formed in 1905 and including amongst its Directors the Hon FC Stanley, brother of the SLT Chairman. It is likely that the Bolton vehicle came from the same source, and for the same reason: they had proved unsuitable for work in the Capital.

More significantly, one imagines, Bolton's Manager Arthur Day would have wondered at the implications of an advertisement which appeared in his September 16th 1905 issue of the trade press, placed by the Receiver of the South Lancashire Tramways Company and offering the Company for sale by Private Tender. Since Bolton, Farnworth and SLT were working jointly, the potential problems were clear to see. The story of that sale and the subsequent formation of Lancashire United is covered in detail in *Lancashire United* by Venture Publications, published in 2006 to mark the Centenary of LUT's formation.

Bolton's first bus was this Stirling single-decker, which could carry twelve seated passengers. Its purchase, for the sum of £750, was evidently arranged by a local man, JV Madgwick. The vehicle was equipped with a 12hp engine which meant it was underpowered, especially on the uneven roads and steep hills in the Borough. Scrutiny of the advertisement overleaf will reveal a representation of this type of vehicle amongst those on offer. The body design is clearly based on current horse bus practice. *(66 Group)*

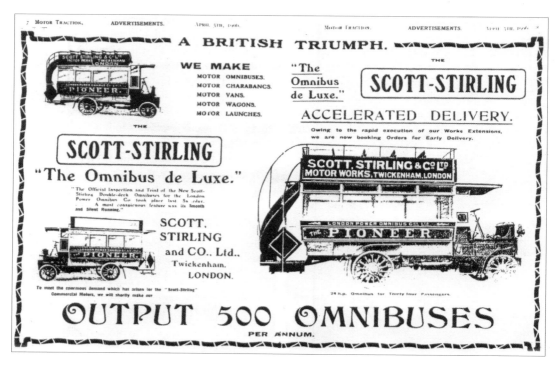

This advert gives the impression of a thriving concern but by 1907 it would have gone out of business. Based at Twickenham, it was assembling buses, and had supplied a large order to the London Power Omnibus Company. They were unable to cope with the traffic available and found their way onto the second-hand market, with three going to Bolton's neighbour Lancashire United Tramways. This could well explain how Bolton became aware of them, but both Bolton and LUT were soon to dispose of them. *(STA)*

Meanwhile expansion of the electric tramway continued. The Toothill Bridge tram tracks were extended to Breightmet on 18th March 1905 and joined the Bury system on 20th May 1907 when through-running commenced. A procession of cars, led by an illuminated Bolton open-topper, is reputed to have then travelled from Bolton to Belle Vue, Manchester, via Bury, to mark the occasion and visit some event at the Pleasure Gardens. Joint operation then involved the two corporation's cars each visiting the other's territory, although, strangely, there seem to be very few photographs of this daily occurrence. One known photograph shows a Bolton football special car loading in Bury, and Bury cars would bring spectators to see Wanderers playing.

Decorated cars also ran to other towns on special occasions, including a visit to Leigh by the above-mentioned car later during 1907, and after suitable modification to the wording of the displays. Decorated cars from Bolton's fleet also appeared in Bury, and in Oldham during World War I in connection with a recruiting drive. In 1927 yet another car was decorated to run in Bolton to commemorate the centenary of the death of Samuel Crompton. Definitely the last car to be officially decorated was No. 440 which marked the end of the Borough's trams as recorded later in our narrative.

In June 1905 the Tramways Committee agreed to grant four day's holiday with pay to the drivers, conductors and night shedmen. Although they worked a long week with few or no breaks conditions were starting, very slowly, to improve.

In July 1905 passengers on the Daubhill and Deane cars were allowed to transfer in Newport Street to cars going to Trinity Street, without payment of additional fares. The route from Farnworth to Walkden was opened and from 1st April 1906, Farnworth leased the tracks, depot and rolling stock to South Lancashire Tramways. The Daubhill service was extended to Four Lane Ends on 19th July 1906 and ten more Brush four-wheel cars were purchased, being numbered 87-96.

In 1906 after the purchase of SLT from the receivers by its Chairman, and the necessary

BOLTON TO BURY - MAY - 1907

Illuminated Car.
1907.
(Copyright)

The use of illuminated trams, still to be seen in Blackpool today, could be found in Bolton 100 years ago. The opening of the service to Bury in May 1907 was the opportunity to decorate No. 46, which is seen on the previous page. Later in the year the same tram, with suitably modified display, visited Leigh and is seen in the upper picture. Bury was to enjoy the subsequent visit of a further illuminated tram to celebrate a shopping week and the car is seen here below in the Rochdale Road depot of Bury Corporation at this time. *(66 Group)*

refinancing had taken place, the new Lancashire United Tramways company acquired a controlling interest in the New St Helens & District Tramways Co Ltd, and also took over the lease of the Farnworth system, and its trams. Back home, and reflecting the growing importance of Bolton's tramways department, the Tramway Offices in Bradshawgate were opened in December 1906. There was little doubt that the 'Worthy Fathers' recognised the tramway as an asset to the Borough, and a tool which they could use to develop and strengthen its trading position, and for this reason expenditure on expansion and upgrading was seen as sensible and a form of investment.

Undaunted by the previous problems with the Stirling bus it was decided to try again and a Darracq-Serpollet steam bus was purchased at a cost of £1,025 for operation on the same route as the previous vehicle, but this too was not successful and was replaced the following year. No doubt if Fred Dibnah had been around in those days he would have applied his enthusiasm to the vehicle and may even have come up with a solution, although the poor condition of the roads was usually the major consideration. The steam bus was replaced by two vehicles, one Commer and one Straker petrol-electric bus, both hired for a year from a London dealer, but while the latter vehicle was destroyed by fire in July 1908, the Commer was purchased for the sum of £740 plus tyres. It continued to operate on the two routes until they were converted to trams, as detailed below. There was then no further bus operation for 12 years.

There must have been some issue with insurance concerning the burnt-out Straker bus for, in December 1909, *Tramway & Railway World* was reporting that Sir Clifton Robinson, Chairman of the other LUT – London United Tramways – was acting as arbitrator to decide who was liable for meeting the cost of this misfortune.

In 1907 it was reported that the Clifton Light Railway had passed its official Board of Trade inspection, and it was opened on 28th February. This allowed trams to travel between Farnworth Black Horse and Clifton. Later in the year Bolton's first section of tramway to be abandoned was the Lee Lane section in Horwich which ceased to operate in December 1907.

Although the connection with SLT which had been used for the procession from Liverpool allowed access for cars from Leigh and Atherton into the centre of Bolton, it was not until 1909

Shiffnall Street Depot and Works

The main depot foundation stone was laid by the Mayor Alderman JE Scowcroft on 11th September 1899 on the site of the old horse tram sheds. The building was 300ft long by 90ft wide with accommodation for some 80 tramcars. There was a 9ft 6in difference in levels between the two sections inside although there was a track connection via Carlton Street. *(66 Group)*

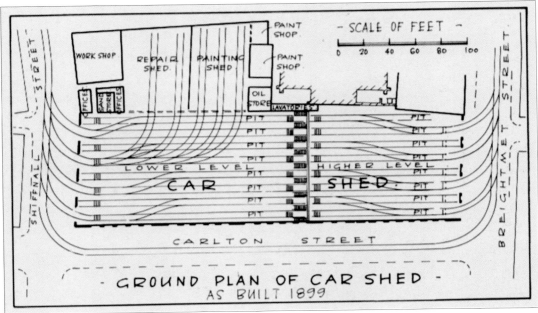

There is confusion surrounding Bolton's second motorbus, BN 229, delivered in 1907, apparently another steam vehicle, this time built by Darracq-Serpollet. It too failed to impress and was replaced the following year. We have been unable to verify whether the registration number was transferred to the above vehicle, as did happen, or whether the Council Minutes are inaccurate, as is also not unknown. Clarification would be welcomed care of the Publishers. *(66 Group)*

As replacements for the unsuccessful steam bus, two buses were hired from a London dealer. The first, LN 9397 seen below, was a Straker-Squire petrol-electric vehicle which had a short life with Bolton, being destroyed by fire in July 1908. *(66 Group)*

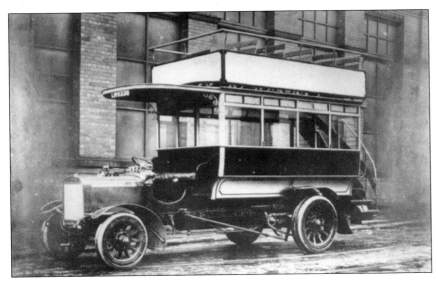

The other hired bus was LN 9398, above, a Commer which was later purchased by the Corporation. It must have impressed because in 1909 a further Commer, but this time a tower wagon, was purchased for access to the overhead line for maintenance, and is seen below with driver Harry Parker and Messrs Charlesworth and Ayres. Use of motor vehicles of this type allowed the overhead men to get to trouble-spots when the lines were blocked by stranded trams or at other busy times. *(66 Group)*

that trams actually ran through in service, and then it was necessary to re-book at the Borough boundary. Furthermore it was a one-sided situation, for Bolton's cars reversed at Four Lane Ends before dropping back down the hill to home. Perhaps there was an insurance issue if the two municipalities were using one company and SLT was using another? The Leigh-Bolton service was abruptly severed in December 1915 as a temporary wartime measure – it was not restored until 1927 so perhaps no-one had heard the all-clear. Eventually, however, in 1909 an agreement was reached with South Lancashire Tramways to allow through running from Bolton via Moses Gate and Farnworth to Clifton and also from Bolton to Lowton via Four Lane Ends, Atherton and Leigh. From June that year SLT trams had been running though from Atherton to Swinton, Walkden and Farnworth via Tyldesley and Mosley Common in what in later years would become one of, if not the, longest trolleybus routes in the country.

One of SLT's Bolton-bound cars had quite a spectacular accident in September 1909 when it left the rails, ran across the road, then the footpath, through a fence and finished up in a field, still upright. The passengers had kept their seats and no one was hurt. Such noteworthy accidents were rare, but derailments on a system whose rails were laid in roads which were continually subsiding as the coal was extracted (far) below were by no means uncommon. The iniquity was that the cost of re-instating the track fell to the tramway operator, and there was no compensation.

In October 1909 the members of the Municipal Tramways & Transport Association met for their Annual Conference and found common ground on items affecting systems throughout the country. The price of traction electricity, interference from Councillors and the cost of reinstating tram tracks affected by subsidence were just three of the burning issues on many Manager's agendas – Bolton did seem to be faring better than many certainly so far as the first two were concerned.

Brighton's Manager was commenting on his undertaking's trading loss, and made the point quite strongly that "the excessive price paid for electric current is crippling the undertaking to such an extent that it will never pay its way until a substantial reduction is obtained". His was far from a lone voice and north of the border one RS Pilcher was fighting the same battle in Aberdeen.

Thirty years later he was still fighting the same battle, but by then in Manchester!

As already mentioned Bolton was pursuing a policy of investing in its transport system, making it a fundamental part of the growth and well-being of the Borough. Thus the cost of power for the trams was kept to a sensible minimum, allowing the Transport Department to create a healthy surplus which could then make a useful contribution to the local rates.

In this year, 1909, the trams carried 26 million passengers over 2½ million car miles, and contributed £6,097 to the rate fund after payment of all charges including depreciation. This was at a time when the cotton industry, the main local employer, was going through a very bad time and nearly all businesses were finding trading very hard. The various tramway manufacturers posted their Annual Results during the autumn each year and with the exception of Brush, which had a full order book, all were reporting reduced profits, shortage of orders and poor prospects for the immediate future. Bolton was fortunate that it had a wide spread of types of business, giving some evening-out, and these Tramways Department results must have been very gratifying. Many other tramway undertakings were showing a loss and having to draw on reserves. In the same year the Bridgeman Street depot was opened. Originally designed to hold 48 cars it was later extended to hold 64 to cope with the growing fleet. Work also commenced during this year on the Carlton Street overhaul workshops.

Meanwhile a Commer tower wagon for use by those working on the overhead wiring was purchased at the end of the year as the need to service the busy tramway became more pressing. By the end of that same year winter had come with a vengeance and *Tramway World* was reporting that tramway traffic in South-East Lancashire had been badly disrupted as a result of gales and heavy snow falls – the Department's snow plough would have been particularly busy after that episode – falls of between 9 and 16ins of snow being followed, inevitably, by serious flooding.

After the drama of the winter, an even worse disaster took place in 1910 when, in a terrible accident at the Pretoria Mine in Atherton, 344 miners lost their lives. Driver John Wright, recalling the event years later, remembered that the following morning not one passenger boarded

This maker's view of car number 81, taken in 1901/2 by the Electric Railway & Carriage Company in Preston, shows how the preserved No. 66 would have looked when new. It is mounted on Brill 22E-type bogies and had two 25hp motors. Travelling to and from work in the dark early hours, or late at night, in the rain and snow would only be for the hardy. *(66 Group)*

Another maker's view, this time of the Bolton snow broom. Ordered from the European McGuire Manufacturing Company, which had premises in Bury, the vehicle was built in 1902 by GF Milnes. It had three 25hp motors, two for propulsion and one to drive the brushes – and was guaranteed to be capable of clearing 18ins of snow from the tracks. A broadly similar vehicle can be seen in the National Tramway Museum collection at Crich, near Matlock in Derbyshire. *(66 Group)*

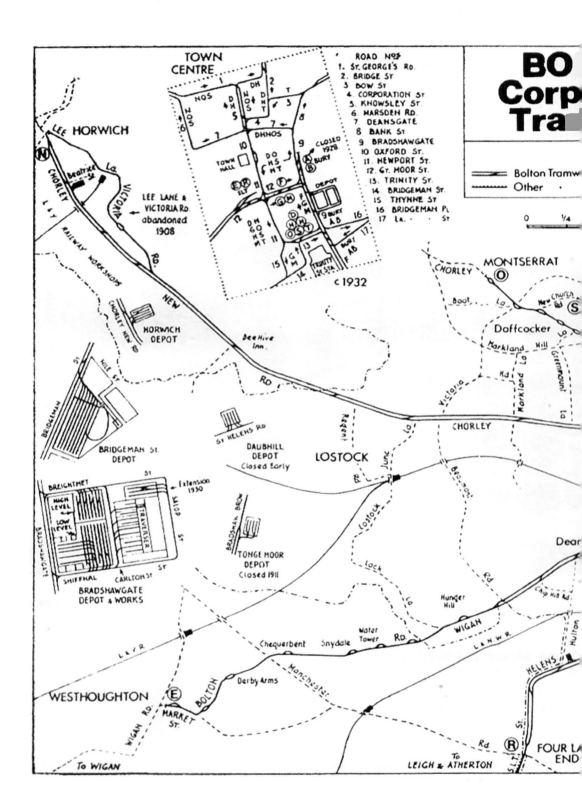

TOWN CENTRE

ROAD Nºs
1. ST. GEORGE'S RD.
2. BRIDGE ST.
3. BOW ST.
4. CORPORATION ST.
5. KNOWSLEY ST.
6. MARSDEN RD.
7. DEANSGATE
8. BANK ST.
9. BRADSHAWGATE
10. OXFORD ST.
11. NEWPORT ST.
12. GT. MOOR ST.
13. TRINITY ST.
14. BRIDGEMAN ST.
15. THYNNE ST.
16. BRIDGEMAN PL.
17. ____ LA. ST.

BO
Corp
Tra

Bolton Tramw
Other

0 ¼

c 1932

LEE HORWICH

Beatrice St.

CHORLEY

LEE LANE & VICTORIA RD. abandoned 1908

RAILWAY WORKSHOPS

CHORLEY NEW RD

HORWICH DEPOT

Bee Hive Inn

BEE HIVE RD

BRIDGEMAN ST.

St. HELENS RD

DAUBHILL DEPOT
Closed Early

BRIDGEMAN ST. DEPOT

MONTSERRAT

CHORLEY

Boot La.

New Church Rd

Doffcocker

Markland Hill

Markland La

Greenmount La

Victoria La

CHORLEY

LOSTOCK

Regent La

Junc

Lostock La

Beacon Rd

Dear

BREIGHTMET

HIGH LEVEL

LOW LEVEL

TRAVERSER

SHIFFNAL CARLTON ST.

BRADSHAWGATE DEPOT & WORKS

Extension 1930

BRADMAN BROW

TONGE MOOR DEPOT
Closed 1911

Lock La

Hunger Hill

WIGAN

L.N.W.R.

Chip Hill Rd

Hulton St.

L & Y R

Chequerbent Snydale

Water Tower Rd

WESTHOUGHTON

Derby Arms

Manchester Rd

WIGAN RD

BOLTON

MARKET ST.

HELENS St.

FOUR LA
END

To WIGAN

To LEIGH & ATHERTON

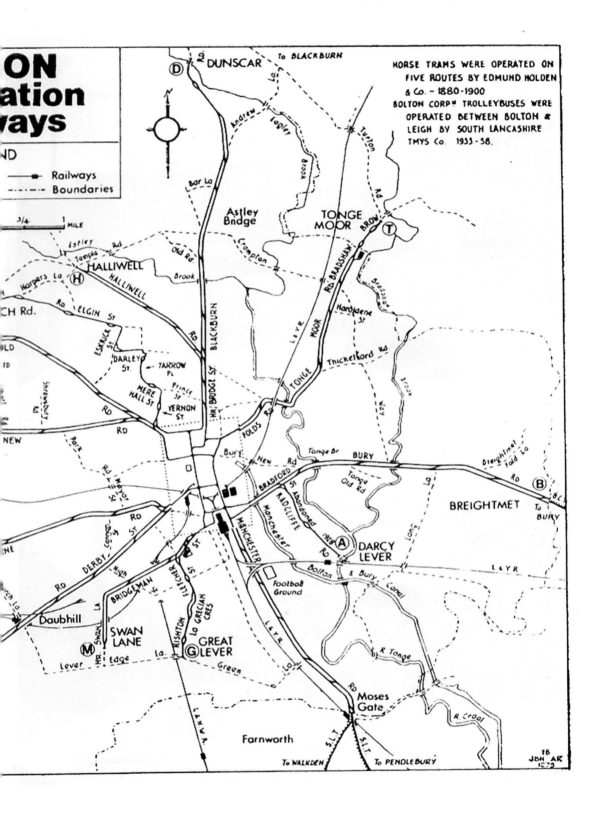

The formal opening of the Darcy Lever route in May 1910 is seen here, the tram being one of the 104-6 batch which were the only single-deckers in the fleet and ran on service A, this being a short branch off the Bury route and which only lasted until March 1928. After withdrawal they found a new use as pavilions in the Borough parks.

This tram, almost certainly No. 48, was so decorated to help raise funds for Oldham tank week in 1917, and is seen here outside the Oldham Corporation depot at Mumps. Such visits by decorated trams to adjacent operators was not unusual, occurring when fundraising was involved or to promote special events, as the Lancashire systems linked with each other at many locations. The work in providing wiring and sockets for the numerous light bulbs would have taken the time of staff with more pressing tasks to occupy them, and loans such as this clearly made a lot of sense. *(66 Group)*

The terminus at Darcy Lever is seen here, on a very wet day, which may have been the final day of operation, although this is unconfirmed. Trams, and earlier buses, were faced with a very steep climb from a standing start – little wonder the early buses were found wanting. See page 46 for a modern bus on the climb. *(66 Group)*

his early morning tram – all had been colliers, and all had been killed.

It was on 6th May 1910 that the Darcy Lever tramway opened, and on 4th May 1911 the Brownlow Fold section commenced operation.

In the 'pipe dreams' file it was noted that The Chorley and District Tramways Limited had issued a prospectus to build a tramway linking Bolton and Preston; the line was to be from the ends of the two corporation systems, but, perhaps not surprisingly, nothing came of this.

Free travel for the blind was introduced in 1910 and in the summers of 1911 and 1912 children's fares were introduced at one penny return except to Horwich which was two pence return for the 12.72 miles   In 1914 waste ticket boxes were fitted to the trams. Speaking to a meeting of the Municipal Tramways and Transport Association some time later, Manager John Barnard explained that Bolton's policy was, wherever possible, to assist the community by keeping the cost of travel stable for those using the trams to-and-from work each day.   How he would have railed against today's competition-at-any-price and the devil-take-the-hindmost situation so often found in our towns and cities.

Following the commencement of World War 1 in 1914 there were no extensions to the system apart from that between Moses Gate and Station Square. Many members of staff had joined the forces and this led to the employment of women as tram conductors. Between 22nd and 24th May 1915 a strike of tramway staff took place as a protest against Saturday overtime.

Perhaps reflecting the satisfactory financial position the Transport Department found itself in, Bolton was one of the few tramway operators which did not take advantage of the Temporary Increase of Fares Act which allowed operators to increase fares for the duration of the war.

From 1915 advertising was allowed on tram vents and by hanging cards in the windows, and this must be around the time that external advertising was discontinued. Perhaps new Manager John Barnard had had some influence here? Although vehicles undoubtedly looked smarter without advertisements it has to be conceded that where advertising was handled properly, and the various displays were not allowed to become faded and untidy, the colourful panels with their distinctive signwriting became very much part of the image.

Model trams from the Edwardian period are always enlivened by such detail. It may be noted here that Salford, which eschewed advertising, insisted that cars from other undertakings running over its tracks should carry no adverts and, accordingly, SLT cars running on the joint service from Walkden to Manchester had to be kept advert-free for this joint through service.

Following the cessation of hostilities in 1918 the *status quo* continued until 1923 when on 8th June an extension of the Chorley Old Road service from Doffcocker to Montserrat was brought into operation. This was followed on 26th October with the opening of the Swan Lane extension.

The maintenance fleet was next extended when a Model 'T' Ford van was purchased, smartly turned out in the department's colours with appropriate lettering, and fitted with an electric arc welding plant for repairs to the tramway track.

In March the following year Bolton's Mayor was in contact with Liverpool with regard to hiring their illuminated tram again. Whether this was done, or whether Bolton's transport workshops produced another of their decorated cars, is uncertain, but certainly an illuminated tram toured the various routes in connection with the Mayor's '300,000 shilling' appeal for Bolton Infirmary, and his Worship was able to report, with thanks, that this had produced £665 – no mean feat. In the same month the Borough Engineer was instructed to proceed with relaying the Chorley Old Road tram tracks, together with part of the Deane route. Rail hardening was also to be investigated for the heavily used sections.

Nineteen-twenty-four was quite a momentous year for the transport department, for that year John Barnard was elected President of the MTTA (later MPTA) and in addition to his job of running the transport system he had various official duties to perform for the Association. In June 1924 he led a party of members to the annual gathering in Paris of the International Union of Tramways, Light Railways and Public Omnibuses (later UITP). In presenting fraternal greetings to his hosts at the conference he took the opportunity to suggest that he might be able to persuade more of his members to make such visits if all the technical papers were not printed only in French! Since only Glasgow and Leeds were represented – in addition to Bolton of course – perhaps the point was not lost on those listening. When Manchester's Stuart Pilcher made a similar visit in the same capacity in 1930 he managed to persuade 35 persons to accompany him, including General Managers from 18 British systems. He did, however, have a trump card: Pilcher laid on a

The use of a non-rail bound vehicle in the maintenance fleet was a logical step, but not one taken by all operators. Furthermore the vehicle was new, bought specifically for the purpose, and not, as might be expected, a worn-out former bus or wartime cast-off. *(GLC)*

brand-new Crossley double-decker from his fleet with, reputedly, Waring & Gillow seating for the trip, and provided door-to-door transport from Manchester to Paris and back on this vehicle.

Back home, in October, the Annual MTTA Conference was well attended, with some 250 delegates and their ladies present. Such was the turnout that Bolton, somewhat to its chagrin, was unable to provide sufficient suitable hotel accommodation, and nearby Southport gallantly came to the rescue. The party was transported by

John Barnard, MBE, Bolton's Tramway Manager from 1913 until he died in 1936. He had joined the department as a clerk in 1900, steadily working his way up until he became Manager. *(STA)*

In 1929 a shopping week took place and the *Bolton Evening News* recorded the event. In the middle distance of this lively scene there is a tram on the Bury route, having just turned at the Bury 'loop', as it was termed, which was in fact a siding in Bradshawgate with a facing crossover. Also to be seen in the original are more steam lorries which were, of course, an everyday part of the scene. *(66 Group)*

This is the stub end terminus of the N route at the Crown Hotel at Horwich in the summer of 1938, with two trams on a curved section of track which was originally part of a loop around Horwich via Lee Lane and Victoria Road. This was abandoned in 1908, the remainder of the route lasting until 1946. Rebuilding of the upper-deck has done away with the top deck bulkhead and open balconies but the driver is still in the open. *(66 Group)*

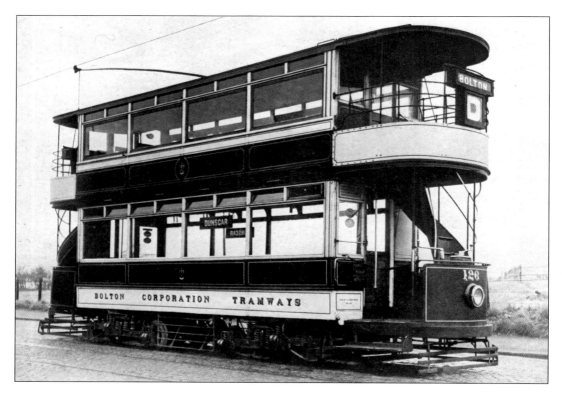

buses back to Bolton, and visits were arranged to world-renowned local clothing manufacturer Tootal Broadhurst Lee, in addition to the Corporation's electricity generating station and transport workshops. The return journey on the second day took in the English Electric Company's works in Preston where most of Bolton's trams were produced. The conference provided a useful forum for discussion on a variety of topics.

Two tramway extensions took place in 1924 when the Brownlow Fold route was extended from Elgin Street to Church Road on 11th April and the Deane service was extended to Westhoughton on 19th December. This latter line, single-track with passing loops, was laid on one side of the road so that should doubling later become necessary disruption would be kept to a minimum.

The additional rolling stock needed by these extensions came as somewhat of a surprise when eight 4-wheel balcony cars which had been new in 1920 were purchased from the Sunderland District Tramway Company prior to that Company converting to bus operation in 1925. The decision to abandon this system was taken in the light of the cost of relaying tracks badly affected by mining subsidence, in addition to generally life-expired

Car 126, seen when new in 1923, could be described as a quintessential Lancashire bogie car – a large double-deck double-truck car with open balconies and normal staircases. It would not have looked out of place in Blackpool, Salford or Manchester, and would be very much at home working with the similar SLT cars when they operated alongside each other in Bolton's streets. *(66 Group)*

FOR SALE.

TRAMWAY CARS FOR SALE.

The Sunderland District Electric Tramways, Ltd.

The above Company has for disposal a number of complete Tramcars. The bodies are Double-Deck with closed-in Upper Saloon. The equipments are B.T.H. G.E.67 and G.E.58. The Trucks are 4 ft. 8½ in. gauge. Arrangements for full inspection can be made by appointment. A number of these cars have been purchased since the War, and are in excellent condition, and can be disposed of as an absolute bargain for prompt delivery. All communications should be addressed :

    G. STRATTON,
      General Manager,
        Sunderland District Electric Tramways,
          Philadelphia, Co. Durham.

NOTE.—In addition to the above, there will be a quantity of other Tramway Plant and Material for disposal in the near future.

infrastructure following unavoidable wartime neglect. Advertised as 'an absolute bargain' they were quickly snapped up by John Barnard's department and gave nine years service, clearly a very sound investment. This really marked the end of tramway development in Bolton, save for rebuilding of cars to enclosed top-deck form, and the acquisition of the eight second-hand former SLT and Farnworth UDC cars from SLT in 1933.

One of the former Sunderland District trams acquired in 1924 commensurate with the extension of the Brownlow Fold route to Church Road is seen above, and makes an interesting comparison with a standard Bolton four-wheel car below, particularly in regard to the treatment of the top-deck window arrangement. The standard Bolton car had six full length drop-down windows, while the ex-Sunderland cars had four fixed windows with quarter lights. They ran almost exclusively on route S to Church Road and when this service was converted in 1933 they were among the first trams to be scrapped. The upper view shows very clearly the exposed nature of the driver's platform, with no protection from the weather and a standing position. Some systems did supply a small jockey seat for their drivers but the manual effort required to stop a large fully-laden tram with just a handbrake meant that sitting was not always an option. Note the horse-drawn delivery cart behind the tram in the top picture. Magee, Marshall & Company have long gone but Cadbury and Hovis are still instantly recognisable names today. *(NTM both)*

Four photographs taken to accompany an article in *Tramway and Railway World* dated October 1924 describing the facilities in the Shiffnall Street depot and workshops which members of the MTTA had seen during their visit which their President John Barnard had arranged. Above is the machine shop, below the bodyshop.

Careful examination of the view above shows the two levels in Shiffnall Street, the upper-level at the rear being occupied by balcony double-deckers and what appears to be an example from the works fleet. Scrutiny of the diagram on page 25 will reveal that access to the workshops was from the main shed, but with the tracks crossing the open pits at right angles. Below can be seen the truck shop – the spaciousness of the complex is noteworthy. *(STA from Tramway & Railway World all)*

Car 41 stands at Walkden Monument, ready to return to Bolton via Moses Gate. The A6 trunk road from London to Scotland, passing through Manchester and Chorley, crosses from left to right behind the tram. The conductor is part way up the staircase on his way to change the indicator, but has stopped for a word with his driver.

The conductor turns the trolley once more as he and the driver prepare for the return from Tonge Moor. Number 12 now sports a fully-enclosed top cover to Bolton's standard pattern, constructed and fitted in the department's own workshops. *(66 Group)*

Bury's number 15 is seen in Bradshawgate, Bolton, awaiting its return home. Joint working had begun as far back as 1907 as seen earlier in the book but this photograph was taken around 1933, shortly before the service finished, and the sight of the cars of the two municipalities working into each other's town centres would cease. Below, Bolton car 95, working a football special, helps move some of the large waiting crowd after a match at Bury's Gigg Lane ground. *(NTM upper, 66 Group lower)*

Tram No. 68 is seen above standing at the Westhoughton terminus, some five and a half miles from Bolton. By pure coincidence, adjoining both terminal points were public houses called the 'Wheatsheaf'. *(66 Group)*

The Falcon Mill at Halliwell (right) was built in 1906 and still exists today, now listed, being a good example of a typical cotton mill. Production ceased c1990 and it is now used by a number of small firms for a variety of purposes. In their heyday the mills provided significant employment, and many were situated close to main tram arteries, thereby supplying plentiful traffic. The low penny tram fare meant that employees no longer had to live in the shadow of the mills, but could enjoy more pleasant living arrangements. At the peak there were around 300 cotton mills locally, the damp Bolton climate being ideal for the spinning of the fine Egyptian yarns for which Bolton was famous. *(DS collection)*

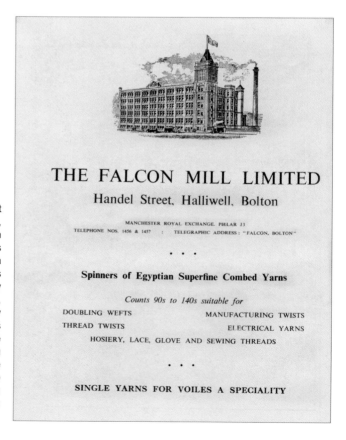

THE FALCON MILL LIMITED

Handel Street, Halliwell, Bolton

MANCHESTER ROYAL EXCHANGE. PIELAR 33
TELEPHONE NOS. 1456 & 1457 : TELEGRAPHIC ADDRESS: "FALCON, BOLTON"

• • •

Spinners of Egyptian Superfine Combed Yarns

Counts 90s to 140s suitable for

DOUBLING WEFTS	MANUFACTURING TWISTS
THREAD TWISTS	ELECTRICAL YARNS

HOSIERY, LACE, GLOVE AND SEWING THREADS

• • •

SINGLE YARNS FOR VOILES A SPECIALITY

Motor Buses –
A Second Attempt

Powers to operate motor buses had been obtained or renewed in 1908, 1914 and 1922 but it was 29th December 1923 before sustained operation commenced. New single-decker buses were purchased in the form of five Leyland bonneted C5 models at a cost of £1,189 each and four Leyland SG9 'side types', where the driver was alongside the engine, at a cost of £1,510 each, and a service to Lowther Street was established. It was soon realised that these C5 buses were underpowered and in September 1924 the Committee accepted a quotation from Leyland Motors to replace the original 30-32hp engines with more powerful 36-40hp units. Additional routes followed on 14th July 1924 between Tudor Avenue and Bury New Road, extended to Ainsworth Lane on New Year's Day 1925.

The trade press announced in November 1924 that Bolton would be promoting a bill in the next session of Parliament to enable them to purchase and operate railless trolley vehicles, and provide motor omnibus services outside the Borough. Although motor bus operation soon extended beyond the boundary, it would be some years before trolleybuses would make their appearance.

The year 1926 saw considerable development of the bus network with new routes commencing on 16th August to Horwich via Chorley Old Road, Belmont, Egerton, Harwood via Tonge Moor Road, Ainsworth and Little Lever via Moses Gate. On 11th October another route commenced, to Darcy Lever, operating alongside the tramway at local fares, and this became the precursor of tramway abandonment, the Darcy Lever trams being withdrawn on 11th March 1928.

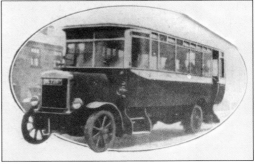

The 1924 delivery of buses, from nearby Leyland Motors Ltd, brought greater reliability, but a marked shortage of power. The five C5 class vehicles, numbered by Bolton as 1-5, were soon re-engined, and their appearance was changed as can be seen in the smaller illustration alongside of No. 4, BN 7267, after conversion when compared to the pre-delivery view of No. 5 below. *(STA both)*

New vehicles purchased for these developments comprised ten Leyland Lion single-deckers and five Leyland Leviathan double-deckers. Whether passengers considered the Leviathans an improvement over the trams might be questionable. With non-pneumatic tyres on indifferent road surfaces the former's ride would be far from smooth whilst the trams were running on tracks which were still in good condition. The Lions were a very different type of vehicle, being the first of the 'modern' vehicles to enter the fleet, and of a type which would soon be familiar throughout the country, and, indeed, in many overseas countries. As a result of these new additions to the fleet, a service to Radcliffe commenced on 21st March 1927.

Number 10, the first LG1 Leviathan, when new in 1926 and before entering service. The short 'cabin' type upper-deck would help reduce the weight on the front axle and keep the total weight within legal limits.

After the small, normal-control, C5 single-deckers, Bolton purchased four examples of Leyland's larger and more powerful SG9 'side-type' model in which the driver sat alongside the engine – these were numbered 6-9. Their appearance was similar to the lower-deck of the Leviathans, though the treatment of the rear, and the doorway arrangements were, of necessity, quite different. *(BCVM)*

The advertisement reproduced above confirms the efforts being made by the tyre manufacturers to keep up with requirements of the bus designers, particularly in so far as increased weight affected the demands placed on the tyres, and also the need to be able to cope with increased speeds which were now permissible. *(STA)*

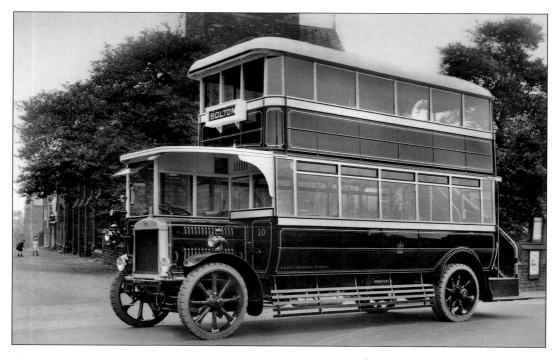

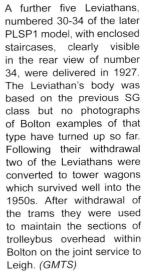

A further five Leviathans, numbered 30-34 of the later PLSP1 model, with enclosed staircases, clearly visible in the rear view of number 34, were delivered in 1927. The Leviathan's body was based on the previous SG class but no photographs of Bolton examples of that type have turned up so far. Following their withdrawal two of the Leviathans were converted to tower wagons which survived well into the 1950s. After withdrawal of the trams they were used to maintain the sections of trolleybus overhead within Bolton on the joint service to Leigh. *(GMTS)*

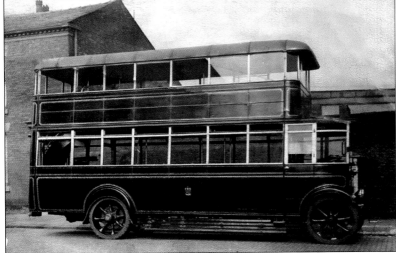

The ten single-deck PLSC1 Lions delivered in 1926 were numbered as 15-24. During 1927/8 seven of the longer PLSC3 model joined the fleet as Nos. 25-9 and 35/6, and, like all the Leylands delivered to that date, had Leyland bodywork. Some of the short Lions were apparently fitted with replacement bodies built by Bolton in 1934. *(GLC)*

When a second batch of five Leviathans arrived in 1927 they were apparently shod with Macintosh Cushion tyres, a half-way house between solids and the pneumatics which at that time would not support the weight of a fully-laden double-decker bus. Most operators converted their Leviathans, and other early vehicles, to pneumatics but this could create problems in exceeding the permitted overall width. Recognising this, the Road Traffic Act gave a dispensation period, and at the expiry of that time most of those veterans – including Bolton's – went to the breakers or were converted for other uses.

The demand for vehicles at this time was such that two vehicles were hired from Leyland Motors Limited in 1927. A Lioness chassis number 45006 and a Leviathan, chassis number 50009, were hired at the rate of £11 per vehicle per week, the Lioness being on hire from 5th April to 8th May and the Leviathan until 11th July.

Leyland's next move was to introduce the revolutionary lowbridge Titan bus, a vehicle whose height had been reduced by a patented side gangway to the upper-deck. Designer GJ Rackham had hit the jackpot for Leyland, and the new model was soon in great demand, partly due to its ability to pass under low railway bridges but also because of its many other attributes, not least of which was its modern appearance. Smooth, quiet running and the ability to carry 51 passengers in covered comfort were amongst the most important

of these. The first Titans had an open rear staircase but when a highbridge demonstrator was built it incorporated an enclosed rear platform, a great improvement. There was, however, a drawback in that the extra weight of the new design meant that only 48 passengers could be carried within the gross weight limit. A further problem arose when Leyland incorporated various emergency exit options into this vehicle, trying to anticipate the forthcoming Road Traffic Act's requirements.

Whilst all this was going on the demand for the new model was such that outside contractors were used by Leyland to meet orders which the Lancashire factory could not supply. Bolton's first ten, numbered 37-46, were genuine Leyland vehicles, as were the next five, numbers 52-56 of which number 54 survives in preservation.

Seen on the Darcy Lever route in 1928, immediately after the replacement of the trams, number 37 was Bolton's first TD1 Titan and was posed for the picture by the maker. As explained in the text it featured a patented design of bodywork, with a side gangway in the upper-deck, which reduced the height sufficient to allow passage beneath low railway bridges. Comparison with the Leviathan of only a couple of years earlier shows how much bus design had suddenly developed. The Titan, and similar models from other manufacturers when they caught up, spelled the death knell for many trams. In the background is St Stephen and All Martyrs Church, now grade one listed, due to its unique construction in terracotta, including some inside fittings. *(STA courtesy BCVM)*

Numbers 57-61 were, like the photographs of No. 6 below show, sub-contracted to Chas Roberts of Horbury, Wakefield, and some were fitted with the enclosed rear. This meant the seating capacity had to be reduced, as mentioned. Leyland were not keen to let the world know that they were subcontracting some orders, and the Roberts order is clearly shown in Leyland's own sales records as having been bodied at Leyland's South Works. The photographs included in these pages clearly show that some at least were built in Wakefield, but whether all of the 52-61 batch were is not clear. Just to compound matters it appears that Leyland applied their body transfer to some vehicles built under licence by others!

By April 1930, Manager John Barnard was negotiating with Leyland for a reduction in price for a further batch of open staircased examples, and it appears that these must have been numbers 5-14. The reduction was against the then-standard price for the then-current enclosed model. Barnard gave his reason to his Transport Committee as

Wakefield-built by Chas Roberts and the last of a batch of five, No. 61 poses for its official portrait at Leyland Motors before delivery to Bolton in May 1930. The open staircase arrangement is clearly visible in this view but the white roof of the earlier deliveries appears to have been replaced by grey. *(BCVM)*

potential issues with the emergency exit on the enclosed models, and it is believed that the worry was that an exit might be approved by the local Watch Committee which might not subsequently meet the Road Traffic Act. Also three seats would be gained by reverting to the open configuration.

The weight problem would re-appear when larger section tyres were fitted, and, even more problematically, they exceed the maximum permissible width of 7ft 6ins. This latter problem was only resolved by a redesign of the chassis members. In an attempt to trim the weight Leyland reduced the floorboard thickness, and also the weight of window glasses, amongst other modifications. Only when the permitted gross vehicle weight was increased was it finally possible to overcome all these issues. Interestingly, some builders, using Leyland drawings and building under licence as sub-contractors, were able to keep within the weight limit but their bodies would not last as long as the Lancashire factory's examples. Much of this information has only come to light, in 2007, from Leyland papers studied by Geoff Lumb in his on-going researches into the General Manager's reports to the main Board. During this brouhaha, and with masterly timing, Rackham moved from Leyland to AEC, leaving someone else to sort out the problems!

Chas Roberts posed their vehicles on the weighbridge by the exit from their premises, making it easy to identify what they built where photographs exist. These views of Titan TD1 number 6 were taken in 1931 and show the enclosed version of the body which they were now building. Bolton took ten TD1s that year, its last before the more powerful TD2 model was introduced, but only numbers 5 and 6 were built in Wakefield – the other eight, numbered 7-14, were built back home at Leyland's South Works. White roofs have returned and the vehicle looks very smart in its maroon livery with lining out and double municipal crests.

The use of the numbers 5 and 6 confirms the departure of the single-deck SG9s by now. Bolton's policy on writing down its buses was in contrast to the much longer life it expected – and obtained – from its trams. Whilst it was normal for buses from the 1920s to have quite a short service life, models like the TD1 would still be operating in many fleets until the early 1950s. Not so in Bolton – theirs had all been disposed of by 1938. This policy meant that the age profile of the bus fleet remained commendably low at this time. *(STA all)*

JR Tognarelli

In 1927 competition was building up and one of Bolton's main competitors was JR Tognarelli, an Italian who had come to England in 1904 and was a restaurateur with an ice cream business in Deansgate. By the outbreak of the First World War he had built up a fleet of commercial vehicles which were used for war service and after the war established a fleet of charabancs which became very much a part of the Bolton holiday scene. He became a naturalised Englishman known for his gentleness and generosity.

In April 1927 he applied for licences to operate an express service between Bolton and Manchester, this being at a time when LUT had been negotiating with Salford Corporation over the latter's Parliamentary Bill to operate bus services outside the City boundary. LUT wanted to get into Manchester and an agreement was reached for a joint LUT/Salford bus service which commenced on 11th May 1927 from Moses Gate to Salford Greengate. The service was operated by LUT pending the receipt of powers by Salford to operate outside the City boundary.

Tognarelli received his licence and commenced operation on 16th May 1927 with nine return journeys per day. By 26th May 1927 Bolton, Salford and LUT advertised a joint service from Bolton to Manchester, this being an extension of the LUT/Salford service from Moses Gate.

Tognarelli responded to this with an application to reduce his fares to those of the joint operators who then increased the frequency of their service to 15 minutes with effect from Wednesday 17th August 1927, from which date Bolton and Salford operated on the service with LUT.

Farnworth was left with the legacy of its 1909 Agreement with SLT, and both Bolton and Tognarelli applied for licences to pick up passengers in the area. The application was referred back under the Agreement to SLT who consented to Bolton but not to Tognarelli, an arrangement which received the approval of the Council. Tognarelli pressed on, and both he and the joint operators took out considerable newspaper advertising space to promote their services. In one advert, Tognarelli stated that all his machines were covered by comprehensive insurance and that anyone saying anything to the contrary would be prosecuted.

Two of Tognarelli's fleet captured by one of Leyland's photographers in 1929. Both are Tiger TS1 models, fitted with 6-cylinder engines, and ideal for long-distance work. The first vehicle, WH 1299, with a Harrington parlour-type body with curtains and fitted-out for overnight travel, is clearly lettered for the London-Glasgow service which ran via Manchester and Bolton. Bolton would have had some work to do on this body to make it suitable for bus work when it joined its fleet. The charabanc, WH 1922, passed to Salford Corporation. *(STA courtesy BCVM)*

On 18th December 1927 Tognarelli commenced a 15-minutes frequency despite having been refused permission for this from the Bolton Watch Committee. Arising from this on Wednesday 21st December 1927, Bolton Council refused to renew Tognarelli's licence, but he continued to operate pending the outcome of an appeal to the Ministry of Transport. The appeal was heard on 17th January 1928 at Bolton and whilst he was refused a licence for a 15-minutes service, his licence for the 30-minutes service was restored. The 30-minutes service commenced on 17th February 1928 with application being made for a 15 minutes service on Saturdays and Sundays and for permission to pick up within Bolton Borough. These were refused.

Conductors were not required on express services and Tognarelli duly economised by using them between Farnworth and Bolton only.

It was something of a surprise, though surely not unconnected with the forthcoming Road Traffic Act, when in 1929, Tognarelli approached Lancashire United Transport to enquire as to whether they would be interested in purchasing his business. He was now operating three routes, Bolton to Manchester, Little Hulton to Manchester via Walkden and Eccles, and Chadderton to Manchester. His fleet comprised 26 vehicles which he valued at £31,000 plus spares valued at £1,000 plus goodwill and his booking office in Bolton at £7,000 giving a total of £39,000. This was considered too high and a revised valuation was received on 27th September quoting vehicles at £26,700 plus spares, goodwill and booking

office at £7,000 giving a total of £33,700. LUT offered Tognarelli £20,000 for his vehicles but at a meeting with Mr EH Edwardes, General Manager of LUT, Tognarelli stated that he was willing to sell but not to give the business away. On 4th November Tognarelli accepted an offer of £24,000 with £500 in spares also being offered. The business was purchased by LUT, Manchester, Salford, Bolton and Oldham. The services were to be taken over from midnight on 8th December 1929. Bolton's contribution to the Tognarelli purchase was £2,181 16s 4d and they received 2 vehicles, WH 1353 an ADC 32 seater and WH 1299 a Leyland TS1 with a 26 seater Harrington body. Both dated from 1928 but the former was in such poor condition that it did not operate for Bolton. This explains the existence of Bolton registered vehicles in the LUT and Salford fleets.

Prior to this deal being finalised it had been reported that Tognarelli planned to build a garage at Manchester Road, Bolton to accommodate 100 buses – clearly he had had the will, the intention, and the finance to take his ambitions to fruition. Herbert Morrison's 1930 Act was almost certainly the final straw for him.

A Bolton-bound LUT single-decker operating one of the cross town services from Hyde c1929 (see text opposite). It neatly illustrates the slow loading arrangement of the narrow, porch-type entrance, with bowler-hatted businessmen forming a decidedly ungentlemanly scrum in the attempt to board. In the rear window the prinicipal stages are shown as Pendlebury, Manchester, Belle Vue (as the picture) and Hyde. The long roof board adds Victoria Bridge as the Manchester pick-up point. (EO collection)

Inter-Urban Express Services

Going back to 1926 Henry Mattinson, the General Manager of Manchester Corporation Transport Department, had been worried about the effect which the growing number of bus operators could have on his tramway system by operating services in parallel with the trams. He decided that if there was a market for fast inter urban bus services, these should be operated by the municipalities.

Manchester commenced a number of 'cross city' services in 1927 and this aroused the interest of neighbouring municipalities and several sought powers to operate bus services beyond their boundaries. One of these was Bolton who, as previously mentioned, in conjunction with Salford and LUT, commenced a service between Bolton and Salford.

In August 1927, Oldham Tramways Committee, encouraged by Manchester, called a General Managers' Conference to discuss the developing situation and plan the way ahead. This was attended by Manchester, Salford, Rochdale, Bury, Bolton, Oldham, Ashton-under-Lyne, Stockport and the Stalybridge, Hyde, Mossley and Dukinfield Joint Tramways and Electricity Board (SHMD Board). On 2nd September it was reported that all present had expressed interest in the operation of through services between Manchester and the various towns represented. One of the principles was that the routes would be across Manchester with no termination in the city centre.

Bolton's involvement in the scheme commenced on 2nd January 1928 with a service from Bolton to Hyde via Salford, Manchester and Denton. (Some sources quote service being extended from Salford to Hyde on 23rd July 1928.) The operators, in addition to Bolton, were Manchester, Lancashire United, Salford and SHMD Board.

Although many other services were developed, this was the only one in which Bolton had an interest. The arrangement was called 'The Coordinated Motor Bus Services Scheme' and full details of the services are given in the book *The Manchester Bus* by Michael Eyre and Chris. Heaps, published by TPC in 1989.

Services outside this scheme were operated by Bolton to Wigan, joint with Wigan Corporation, via Westhoughton and Lostock commencing on 1st September 1927. The proposals for this service had attracted objections from the London, Midland and Scottish Railway Company and this resulted in a sitting before the Traffic Commissioners in Manchester. When it was explained that the proposed service was designed to meet the needs of local traffic on the outskirts of Bolton and Wigan, and an assurance given that it was not an express service, the objection from the Railway Company was withdrawn. This was followed on 1st January 1928 by a service to Warrington operated in conjunction with Lancashire United Transport although the entire service was operated by LUT buses. It seems that cooperation between Bolton and Lancashire United was good. Perhaps former Traffic Manager Harry England's presence helped.

Freeman's Silver Star

On 26th March 1930, Mr Frank Green, the owner of Freeman's Silver Star Service whose operations included a route between Chorley and Bolton, visited Mr Barnard, the Bolton General Manager, to enquire as to whether or not Bolton would be interested in purchasing the business. Arising from this, a meeting was arranged with Ribble for 1st April to discuss the matter further but nothing came from it. Mr Green was later declared bankrupt and several vehicles from his fleet were repossessed by the finance company. The buses were then transferred to Mrs Green under a new hire purchase agreement and she then employed her husband to operate a partial service from July.

By October the buses had again been repossessed and the trustees then applied for the Freeman licences to be transferred to them following purchase of the five vehicles, including one Leyland Titan double-decker, from the finance company. On 18th October the new licences were issued to the trustees. On Tuesday 4th November there was a telephone call from Major Hickmott of Ribble informing Bolton that Ribble had purchased Freemans Silver Star from the Trustees of Freemans with effect from midnight on that day for the sum of £7,500 which included 13 vehicles. Following several discussions, the Ribble Board agreed to Bolton purchasing the goodwill of Freemans between Horwich and Bolton to enable

Freeman's SG11 single-deckers were very similar in appearance to the Bolton SG9s of which we have no pictures. Their Titan TD1, TE 2943, also shown here, was a former Leyland demonstrator and it would appear these and Freeman's other vehicles led an eventful life, to be sold, operated and repossessed several times in their lives. These two ended their days with Ribble after Bolton declined the offer to buy the ailing concern.
(STA courtesy BCVM)

the route to be operated on a 50/50 basis rather than three fifths Ribble and two fifths Bolton. The sum of £1,000 was paid for the goodwill and whilst Bolton had no desire to purchase a vehicle, they decided, apparently as a diplomatic gesture, to purchase one of the Leyland Tiger single-deckers – TE 8290 – for £960.

This was not the end of the saga, however, for on 17th November the Freeman family decided to apply for licences to operate services similar to those which had been sold because the family were the primary creditors of the bus service and it had been sold without their knowledge. The licence was not granted.

Another important event of 1930 was the transfer of the town's main bus terminus from Victoria Square to what was to become Moor Lane Bus Station. The site had previously been occupied by Bessemers Forge Steel Works which closed in 1924. Adjacent was the Corporation Gas Works, and some terraced houses, and then, literally just across the road, the Town Hall. Business certainly took precedence in those days, and the selection of noxious smells inside the Town Hall must have been quite something.

An agreement with Ribble Motor Services in 1931 then stabilised the position regarding that operator's services into Bolton. It has been said that Ribble found Bolton and St Helens to be cooperative when it came to discussing agreements within their boundaries. Ribble was far less cooperative with LUT at this time.

Express Service Problems

The express services across Manchester were doing well, the Hyde service carrying 3.5 million passengers in 1931, to the extent that complaints were received from a number of sources. In 1931 the Chief Constable of Manchester complained of traffic congestion particularly in Market Street and directed that the services be kept away from Market Street and also that they did not wait in the City Centre. There were also complaints from taxi owners regarding congestion and from the railways who claimed to be losing revenue to the express bus services. In an attempt to address these complaints, many of the services were split in Manchester City Centre, in some cases involving a walk between the terminus of the southern section and the terminus of the northern section. In a world where nothing really changes, 75 years later the letters columns of *The Manchester Evening News* have carried extensive footage from readers complaining that they have a long walk from the Shudehill interchange to Piccadilly if they need a cross-town connection.

The Bolton to Hyde service was split on 1st February 1933, and both sections retained the originally allocated service number 8. The northern section terminated in Victoria Bus Station, Salford, and the southern section in Piccadilly. The Hyde tram service was extended from Piccadilly to Exchange to provide a link between the two sections. It seems that the police were willing to accept the trams operating in Market Street, but not the express buses. The northern section retained the number 8 into Greater Manchester Transport days and the southern section was absorbed into the new service 125, Manchester-Hyde-Glossop in 1948 when the Hyde trams ceased operation.

In the background, Bolton Parish Church, built in 1870, looks down in 1932 on the Deansgate, Bradshawgate, Churchgate and Bank Street junction and the site of the original Market Cross seen here with its more modern replacement. Leyland Titan bus No. 10 is operating on service 10 en route to Markland Hill from Crompton Way. *(STA courtesy BCVM)*

Domestic Events back in Bolton

In 1928 the average distance that could be travelled on the trams for a fare of one penny was 1 mile 974 yards and children under 13 years in school holidays could travel any distance on any route for one halfpenny except to Horwich where the fare was one penny.

The points at Knowsley Street / Oxford Street junction which had been operated by a 'points boy' who had to go into the middle of the road to perform the operation, were modified by the installation of a box on the pavement containing levers. These were made automatic in 1931/32, operation being activated by the tram's driver either drawing current, or coasting, as he approached the points.

The Bridgeman Street shed had been extended in 1927, and in October 1929 a new bus garage was opened in Crook Street. Also in 1929 new bus services were commenced to Barrow Bridge, to New Hall Lane and to Crompton Way, together with express services to Rochdale via Bury and to Manchester via Little Hulton. The Rochdale service carried a 'T' suffix to the route number in order to fit in with the Rochdale system whereby services entering the town centre via Tweedale Street carried the 'T' suffix to the route number. When the Bury tram service was withdrawn in 1934 and the express route split, the 'T' suffix was added to the Breightmet number in order to indicate 'through to Bury'.

The Horwich to Westhoughton bus service was extended to Atherton on 6th January 1930 and further extended to Leigh on 16th April 1930. This brought Leigh into the Joint Operation Agreement but the mileage was small and Leigh did not operate on the service.

In 1932 Bolton's livery of maroon with white relief was replaced by maroon with red relief giving a distinctive, if rather drab appearance. This livery was retained until after the Second World War when it was changed to maroon with three cream bands which was a great improvement. Coincidentally, around 1932 Ashton-under-Lyne had also incorporated a deep band of red into its livery, though its vehicles were painted dark blue and white, of course.

In 1933 the road under the railway bridge in Crook Street was lowered to allow double-deck buses to pass beneath it.

Vehicle developments in 1933 included the purchase of an AEC 'Q' type double-decker, a revolutionary design with the engine at the side. The vehicle was not a success and saw little service from 1937 until its withdrawal in 1939. In the same year ten Leyland TD2 and ten Leyland TD3 double-deckers were purchased. The ten TD2 and five of the TD3 vehicles had bodies built by the local firm of Bromilow & Edwards, a firm more commonly associated with the building of tipper trucks, rather than bus bodywork. In June 1933 the firm of Orr of Little Hulton was taken over jointly with Bury and Salford. It is claimed that Orr was one of the more interesting operators of the area who interpreted timetables liberally and had incidents with Salford tramcars which led to the business being wound up.

A 1933 view in Deansgate shows two pristine Bromilow & Edwards-bodied buses, just delivered and in the distinctive new livery, one operating the number 1 from the recently converted S tram route. A tram in the background is working to Horwich. The leading vehicle, No. 65, is a TD2 from a batch of ten – 62-71 – with lowbridge bodywork; behind, No. 74 is one of five highbridge TD3 models – 72-76 – with their instantly recognisable roof profile. Bolton was shopping around at this time, and there would be two Weymann and three English Electric-bodied TD3s when the next new vehicles joined the fleet. *(66 Group)*

Leyland PLSC Lion, number 17, is seen at the top of the page at Barrow Bridge, a village on the northern outskirts of Bolton, and an attraction for those seeking a break away from the town, where access to the '63-steps' would lead to open countryside. Services here began in 1929. Behind the bus are the remains of a cotton mill built in the 1850s, the whole complex being built as an early example of a model industrial village and pre-dating the better-known Port Sunlight. When new it was visited by Prince Albert who gave the project his stamp of approval. *(66 Group)*

Developments in maintenance and increased storage accommodation for the growing bus fleet included this equipment seen above for lifting vehicles to give easier access for work on the chassis. One of the Titans awaits its turn on the elevator. *(GLC)*

The supply of Forest City Electric automatic points, of which Bolton utilised around ten sets, and as promoted by the advertisement alongside, was another example of the fact that in the early years of the 20th Century, Lancashire was part of the workshop of the world. Today Forest City are still well-known as suppliers of automatic traffic lights for road junctions. Another example of a local product being widely used was provided by Philipson of Astley Bridge, a small engineering firm which supplied patented life guards approved by the Board of Trade and fitted to trams in Bolton and elsewhere. *(STA)*

Two views of the Q, designed by GJ Rackham who had been responsible for the Titan when employed by Leyland. The Q was one of his less successful designs for AEC, which he joined in 1928 after leaving the Lancashire builder. The offside view shows the engine position, behind the grilles. Inside the saloon a bench seat covered the power unit, allowing more space for passengers than a conventional design. The bodywork was by Charles Roe of Leeds, and these illustrations were taken by the company's photographer. *(STA)*.

58

Taken in the summer of 1934, at the junction of Great Moor Street and Bradshawgate, the above picture shows Bolton No. 83, one of ten Bromilow & Edwards-bodied TD3s delivered that year, leaving for Breightmet and Bury, the trams having ceased the previous January. Note the revised frontal treatment; the 'piano-front' seen on pages 54/5 has given way to a smoother, unbroken outline. Number 83 was to be rebodied by Northern Coachbuilders soon after the war ended. *(66 Group)*

Bromilow & Edwards were far better known as manufacturers of tipping gear for lorries, rather than bus bodybuilders, and were just one more example of the wide variety of specialist engineering concerns which could be found within the Bolton Borough. *(STA).*

Facing page: The junction of Deansgate crossing with Oxford Street and Knowsley Street seen in 1934 with Bolton's Q, number 2, on route 10 between Markland Hill and Crompton Way. It did not prove successful in Bolton and was sold in 1939. The tram, on the other hand, was one of the last batch bought in 1927 and was working on the Chorley Old Road service to Doffcocker and Montserrat, remaining in the fleet until the end in 1947. Almost hidden is one of Ribble's PLSC Lions bound for Preston. *(STA courtesy BCVM)*

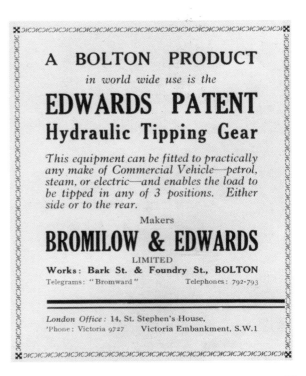

In 1934 Bolton purchased five Leyland Tiger TS6c single-deckers with bodies by HV Burlingham of Blackpool. They were numbered 92-6 and here number 95 is shown when repainted in the post-war livery. Despite the close proximity of Blackpool to Bolton, and the excellent reputation which the seaside coachbuilder had, these were the only Burlingham bodies purchased by Bolton.

The 1935 intake of new vehicles comprised six Leyland TS7c models, three numbered 97-99 with bodies by Massey Brothers which were rebodied as double-deckers after the war, and three numbered 100-102 with metal-framed bodies by Leyland Motors. The last of the Leyland batch, No. 102 is shown. *(STA all)*

Arrival of the Trolleybuses

In 1933 the South Lancashire Transport trolleybus system reached Bolton and on 29th March 1936, as its contribution, Bolton agreed to pay the interest and working costs for four trolleybuses, which after eight years, were to become the property of Bolton Corporation. This brought about the unusual situation of Bolton owning four trolleybuses which operated with SLT livery and legal lettering and were housed and maintained at Atherton. The trade press of the day recorded their arrival, and Leyland, manufacturers of the chassis, were keen to promote their success in securing the order whereas the previous chassis had all been supplied by Guy Motors. The Lancashire company, by then LUT's major motor bus supplier, continued supplying SLT's trolleybus chassis until wartime restrictions brought the association to an end.

The whole situation was rather curious since SLT, as operator, would have been far more involved in the design and specification than Bolton, the owner. The vehicles were fitted with regenerative braking equipment, ideal for the route on which they would operate, with a long climb to Bolton's boundary at Four Lane Ends and then the matching downhill run into the town centre. Ned Edwardes, LUT's Managing Director, had in earlier years been the power station engineer at Atherton, and would have been keenly aware of what these machines could do when braking hard on that long descent – regeneration could put up to 1,000 volts back into the overhead. If Bolton's trams were not to receive a surprise bonus there would need to be a means of absorbing this excess. Derek Shepherd, one-time power station engineer in Bolton, believes the answer may lay in Bolton's huge 550 volt battery, a piece of apparatus which was housed in its own substantial building, and consisted of banks of open glass jars, and would have absorbed this sudden surge.

The term battery is perhaps a misnomer nowadays; at the time it was also referred to as an accumulator, something many households were accustomed to using to power their new wireless sets, and an item which would be taken to the local chemist for re-charging when necessary. The Tudor Accumulator Company supplied many transport undertakings with such batteries, and one supplied to Manchester just for lighting purposes consisted of 210 cells, open jars containing acid and each weighing around three tons, and containing 77 plates approximately 30ins x 20ins. This equipment would be charged during the day and would then be capable of maintaining the supply at night time when demand was less. Before the First War, a traction battery capable of powering the trams off-peak, or in emergency, would normally be housed in a separate building, could cost up to £2,000, and around £500 per annum to maintain – around the price of a four-wheel tramcar.

Unlike the trams, the trolleybuses ran only from Spinning Jenny Street, Leigh, using the terminal which stood on land purchased in 1927 especially for the purpose. After passing the Howe Bridge depot, and power station, they proceeded through Atherton and climbed to the top of the ridge where the Four Lane Ends hotel stood at the Bolton boundary. From there they ran in Bolton's territory to the Howell Croft terminus.

Electricity generation and supply began in 1894 in Bolton, quite early in the national scheme of such events. Like the tramway system, it soon provided a useful source of profitable income for the Borough, having popularised the new medium through the brightly lit electric tramcars passing by houses which were still lit by gas or even candlepower. The second generating station took over from the original one in 1914 and lasted until 1979. Direct current was still supplied to consumers until the 1960s as also was a peculiar single-phase ac system that worked at 2,000 volts 83 cycles instead on the normal 6,600 volts at 50 cycles – all now long forgotten. *(DS collection)*

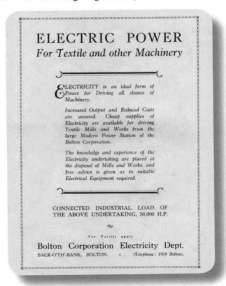

ELECTRIC POWER
For Textile and other Machinery

ELECTRICITY is an ideal form of Power for Driving all classes of Machinery.

Increased Output and Reduced Costs are assured. Cheap supplies of Electricity are available for driving Textile Mills and Works from the large Modern Power Station of the Bolton Corporation.

The knowledge and experience of the Electricity undertaking are placed at the disposal of Mills and Works, and free advice is given as to suitable Electrical Equipment required.

CONNECTED INDUSTRIAL LOAD OF THE ABOVE UNDERTAKING, 50,000 H.P.

For Tariffs apply

Bolton Corporation Electricity Dept.
BACK-O'TH'-BANK, BOLTON.   :   (Telephone: 1970 Bolton).

Photographed when brand new, possibly on its first day in service, this is one of the four Leyland TTB4 Roe-bodied trolleybuses bought by Bolton Corporation and operated by SLT for 22 years on its behalf, following the demise of the Bolton trams on the joint service between Bolton and Leigh in 1936. This was after the conversion of the route from tramcar operation following SLT's abandonment of its tramway back in December 1933. It has just left Howell Croft terminus *en route* for Leigh and is passing the London and North Western Great Moor Street Railway Station, long since demolished. The tram tracks in the picture which previously served the Daubhill route also served the Westhoughton route and remained in use until 1946.

The two views of No. 50 when new were taken at CH Roe's factory in Crossgates, Leeds.
(BCVM upper, STA others)

This official Leyland view of No. 48 shows the first of the four trolleybuses bought by Bolton Corporation. The pale coloured building behind the vehicle is the Art Gallery and Museum in the Crescent behind the Town Hall which, in 1936, was under construction. Howell Croft South where this picture was taken disappeared with redevelopment and was near where the Octagon Theatre and car park are now situated. To the right in the picture of the pedestrian walking towards the camera was the tram siding for the Westhoughton and Daubhill trams which remained in use until December 1946 for the Deane cars. *(STA courtesy BCVM)*

The interior view taken before delivery shows the unusual lower-deck interior layout. The longitudinal seats over the rear bogie are a logical solution to the problem of covering the wheelarches – often referred to as the paddleboxes – but the luggage racks are a less obvious fitment in a vehicle working on a service used largely by workmen. *(STA)*

A wartime view taken outside SLT's Atherton depot, where the Bolton trolleybuses were housed and maintained. In the background can be seen part of the power station complex. The photograph clearly shows the additional white paint applied to aid identification in the blackout although by the time a following driver saw the grimy white stripes it might well have been a little late! The exact date is unknown but lack of normal care and attention common to all fleets as the war progressed is all too obvious. *(STA)*

Bolton's trams ran at c500 volts whereas the SLT trolleybus system was supplied at c550volts; thus the Atherton-bound trolleybuses received a small but noticeable surge of power when they left Four Lane Ends, sending them scurrying down hill and back to Leigh. Traction batteries were fitted and so the failing-light syndrome so noticeable at the end of sections where the earlier Guys were involved did not apply. Riding in the upper-deck of one of those lowbridge vehicles on a dark wet night was quite an experience; after passing under a section feeder there was a sudden spurt of power and all the lights reappeared, only to gradually fade away again towards the next feed point.

These four three-axle vehicles, with highbridge bodywork by Charles Roe of Leeds, carrying SLT fleet numbers 48-51, were to be operated exclusively on the Bolton route, and were joined the following year by a further pair of similar vehicles, numbers 52 and 53 in the SLT fleet and the property of the Atherton company. A curious feature of the Bolton examples was the inclusion of luggage racks above the long longitudinal seats in the lower deck. SLT clearly saw no need for such extravagance, and their two vehicles were not so equipped. After a lifetime shuttling backards and forwards between the two termini the 'Bolton Four', so far as is known, entered a Bolton depot for the first time when they were returned from Atherton to be sold after the closure of the trolleybus service in 1958. They were then disposed of to Birds of Stratford upon Avon for £360. One of the SLT pair, number 53, lasted until the end of that system's operation, providing a reminder of what had previously been operating between Leigh and Bolton.

Tramway Decline

On 1st March 1933, the Church Road Tramway was replaced by a bus service, the tramway having become due for renewal and the bus service was linked with the Lowther Street service to provide a cross town facility. Development of other bus services also proceeded in 1933 and 1934 with the following introductions and also numerous extensions.:-

June 1933 :-	Breightmet - Little Lever
June 1933 :-	Bolton - Little Lever - Radcliffe - Manchester. Ex Orr.
June 1934 :-	Affetside
July 1934 :-	Harwood - Tonge Moor Road
Oct. 1934 :-	Barrow Bridge - Townleys

In January 1934 the Bury tram service ceased and the Rochdale bus service was diverted via Heywood, no longer operated as an express. On 1st July 1934, H Martin of Affetside's business was acquired. He had operated a service from Tonge Moor to Affetside, to Harwood and to Brookfield Lane using a vehicle known as the 'Rocket'.

The 1934 intake of new vehicles comprised ten Leyland TD3c double-deckers and five Leyland TS6c single-deckers. The 'c' suffix indicated that they were fitted with the torque converter transmission system which had recently been introduced by Leyland Motors in an attempt to simplify the driving by eliminating the need for the driver to be involved with gear changing. Buses so fitted normally carried the words 'GEARLESS BUS' on the radiator and the system appealed to municipal operators faced with increasing levels of town traffic and also the need to train tram drivers to drive buses as tram replacement schemes were being introduced. Bolton standardised on this system for all deliveries between 1934 and 1942.

The downside to this drive was that it was less efficient in output terms and in terms of fuel consumption compared to the standard clutch and gearbox arrangement. In view of this a number of operators did replace the torque convertor system with standard clutch and gearbox and in 1953 Bolton carried out such a programme on the remaining 1940-2 vehicles comprising numbers 193-218/22/5-30/2-4/9-42. The system had a lever similar in appearance to a gear lever with 4 positions :- Neutral, Drive, Direct and Reverse. The bus would be started in 'Drive' and having attained a speed of around 20mph, the lever would be moved to the 'Direct' position which was in effect a direct through drive from the engine.

Nineteen-thirty-six was notable for the commencement of total tramway abandonment with the following routes being affected on the dates indicated.

March 1936 :-	Hulton Lane
May 1936 :-	Great Lever
August 1936 :-	Swan Lane
October 1937 :-	Dunscar

Bridgeman Street Tram Depot was converted to a Bus Depot in March 1937.

At its meeting in early February 1938 the Town Council agreed by a large majority to accept the recommendation of the Transport

This picture from the summer of 1939 depicts Tonge Moor Road, with tram No.81 *en route* for Bolton and motorbus No. 80 on service 7, which linked with service 6 to form a circular service. The picture appears to be taken from the front upper-deck of a tram following the motorbus, and despite appearances to the contrary, Tonge Moor Road was still typically paved with stone sets and had not been tarmaced. The fact that the two vehicles, of different types but carrying almost identical fleet numbers explains why a year later, the trams had '300' added to their fleet numbers to help distinguish the two types. Had the war not intervened the trams would have gone by then and there would have been no need for renumbering. *(66 Group)*

Committee to replace all trams by buses. The alternative proposal to substitute trolleybuses was defeated. The trams on the Montserrat service were replaced by buses in January 1939 and those on the Halliwell service in August 1939. Further progress on the abandonment of the tramways had to be postponed because of World War 2, and as a wartime emergency measure trams returned to the Halliwell service on 1st April 1940.

Lewis Cronshaw had operated an express service from Blackburn to Manchester via Bolton since 1927 and this was acquired in 1937 jointly by Bolton, Ribble and Lancashire United. In 1931 the joint operators had applied for a service between Blackburn and Manchester but this had been opposed by Mr Cronshaw and their application was refused. Now that they had this service, a new agreement was entered into by Ribble and Bolton with regard to their three joint operations. Bolton's share of the revenue was to be Blackburn to Bolton 21.2%, Chorley to Bolton 25% and Blackburn to Manchester 19.4%. Bolton did not operate on the Blackburn to Manchester service, but the number X66 was included on Bolton blinds. During the summer months it was common practice for Bolton to work some of Ribble's mileage on the Chorley to Bolton service to enable Ribble vehicles to be used elsewhere. Bolton's contribution to the purchase of the Cronshaw business was £1,802 3s 7d less credit for sold vehicles £271 12s 0d. Bolton inspected Cronshaw's coaches but declined to buy any.

On 11th August 1938 the sudden death occurred, at the age of 64 years, of the General Manager Mr JHO Barnard MBE, following a seizure. General Manager since 1913, he was a well-known figure in the industry. In 1917 he became secretary of the Lancashire and Cheshire Municipal Tramways Association and he was awarded the MBE in the 1920 New Years Honours List. In 1924 he was elected President of the Municipal Tramways Association and in 1935 he was one of a number of Bolton Corporation Officers who received the King's Silver Jubilee Medal. At the time of his death he was Chairman of the National Joint Industrial Council for the Road Passenger Transport Industry. In a tribute to him, published in *Bus and Coach* magazine dated September 1938, Mr Harold E Clay, who, in his Trade Union capacity had often been on opposite sides to Mr Barnard, recalls that he had been very much involved in discussions with the trade unions concerning the training of tram drivers to drive buses. He described him as a man of sound common sense with an extensive knowledge of transport, brusque and blunt, but above all with a broad human understanding and an intensive dislike of sharp practice.

Mr Barnard was succeeded by his deputy Mr Clement Ormrod who had joined the Department 39 years previously as a clerk but, sadly, he died in office in May 1939. Following this, Mr Arthur Arnold Jackson, General Manager and Engineer of St Helens Corporation Transport Department was appointed General Manager and remained in office until he retired on 31st December 1959.

C Ormerod, who was General Manager 1938-9.

AA Jackson, who was General Manager for 20 years.

This picture was taken in 1933 on the Wheatsheaf siding, on the corner of Newport Street, which accommodated the trams on both the Westhoughton and Leigh routes. The former route is being serviced by a four-wheel car, while the decidedly down-at-heel SLT bogie car is showing Leigh Market as its destination. *(NTM)*

Now looking pristine following long-overdue attention ex-SLT and former Farnworth District tram No.39 gleams in its Bolton livery in 1938. These trams migrated to the Farnworth route after the Daubhill route closed in 1936 and stayed on there until its closure in 1944 when they transferred to the Horwich route, staying there until the end of their days. Originally eight in number, two were withdrawn before the war to keep the others going, although the bogies of one were placed under No. 451 (formerly Bury No.55) in order to improve its performance. *(NTM)*

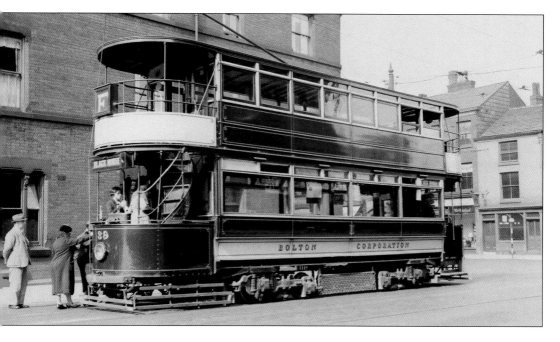

A typical 1930s Bolton tram seen in a 1939 summer view on the Tonge Moor route, crossing Victoria Square and passing the town's War Memorial which still exists, although the other buildings in the view have gone. Cars of this batch migrated to this route after the Chorley Old Road service finished. The tower immediately above the tram was in Hotel Street which belonged to the Gas Company's offices. The overhead wire beyond the tram was provided for a loop which was not normally used other than in emergencies. *(NTM)*

1936 saw a return to double-deckers when 30 Leyland TD4c models were supplied. The first ten had lowbridge bodies by Charles Roberts of Wakefield and No. 15, the first of the ten, is shown in the usual spot on the maker's weighbridge when new. *(RMC)*

Also supplied as part of the 1936 delivery of Titan TD4c models were fifteen with lowbridge bodies by Massey Brothers of Wigan, numbered 30-44. Number 33 is shown when new. *(RMC)*

Two views depicting 1938-built Leyland TS8c torque-convertor fitted Tigers numbers 1 and 4 when new. Number 1 is seen above outside Park Royal's London factory where the first two were built; the other two were built by Massey Bros in Pemberton – number 4 is shown below. The large header tank on the front bulkhead, where the Autovac would normally be housed, clearly indicates the fitting of the torque-convertor transmission which was designed to make bus driving easier for former tram drivers as the trams were withdrawn. In 1949 numbers 3 built by Massey and 96 (page 60), built by Burlingham, exchanged bodies during the rebodying exercises.

Whilst the Massey vehicles were fitted with bus seats the first two saloons were fitted with more comfortable seating, and although still called buses, were treated more like coaches and used by Council Committees for visits and inspections; they were also used for Private Hire work. In 1953 this included the conveyance of a party of Scouts to Mablethorpe to help with the East Coast Flood relief work, the supply of the bus being part of Bolton's contribution to the disaster relief. Derek Shepherd remembers that weekend, and the long journey home where the deep seats allowed welcome sleep. *(STA both).*

Handshakes and farewells as saloon number 1 prepares to leave Thurston Road, Leyland. It was photographed outside the Leyland Motors offices at Leyland, having been used to convey the Transport Committee on a factory visit. The famous South Works where bus body building took place until 1953 is situated at the end of the road. The British Commercial Vehicle Museum now occupies part of that site. *(STA courtesy BCVM)*

The other coach fitted example, No. 2, was photographed in more mundane everyday service in Bolton in August 1957 when 19 years old and shortly before withdrawal. Both views show the change in appearance created by the application of the post-war livery when compared to those on the facing page. *(KWS)*

When East Lancashire Coachbuilders was reconstituted in 1938 with the arrival of Alfred Alcock and George Danson from Massey Brothers, the firm commenced building double-deckers. The first ten to be supplied were for Bolton and were numbered 143-52. Number 145, ABN 407, is shown when new and the similarity between this and the then current Massey design is evident. They were of composite construction, having been produced before the intended metal frame design had been finalised. The deep header tank for the torque convertor made an ideal spot for applying the fleet number. *(STA)*

ABN 623, number 175, was one of 40 Leyland TD5c models supplied in 1939 with Massey Brothers bodies. The Pemberton company's design had changed from the previous year in that the flat sloping front had been replaced by a gently curving front which is evident in this photograph. Six-bay construction was still employed but would give way to 5-bay the following year. The horizontal lower edge to the windscreen is retained whereas some Massey bodies supplied to other operators in 1939 had the curved lower edge. *(RMC)*

Number 239 was one of a batch of Massey-bodied Leyland TD7c models which entered service between 1940 and 1942. The development from the 1939 Massey design is evident with change from 6-bay to 5-bay construction, inclusion of 'D' shaped lower saloon front and rear windows and the curved lower edge to the windscreen. The outswept lower panels also contrast with the 1939 design. This was Massey's final pre-war body design and it was always readily identifiable. *(RMC)*

Fourteen of the Leyland TD4c models supplied in 1937 had metal-framed bodies by Leyland Motors to a design introduced the previous year and of which Bolton had received four lowbridge examples. This was a much sleeker design with gentle curve to the front profile extending from roof level to just above the offside mudguard. The top of the windscreen was lifted to just below the upper-saloon floor level giving an airy and spacious environment to the cab. The upper photograph shows No. 114 and the lower one No. 116, both taken in April 1952 when they had given 15 years service. *(RM both)*

Wartime

Wartime restrictions were quickly imposed in Bolton as they were throughout the country. Services were reduced, lighting in the streets was reduced or eliminated, and vehicles were forced to reduce their own interior lighting by masks and the use of blue bulbs. Headlights were masked to the extent that they were virtually useless and driving of buses became a nightmare in the blackout. These were all necessary precautions against the possibility of providing enemy planes with anything which might constitute a target or provide a clue as to where the planes actually were.

Thankfully, Bolton escaped most of the air raid attacks which caused so much devastation and loss of life in nearby Manchester and Liverpool – even the giant Horwich railway locomotive works was untouched – just stray bombs being jettisoned by German planes heading for home but no real focused attacks. However, travel became a luxury – 'Is your journey really necessary' asked Government posters – and maintenance of vehicles soon suffered as the Department lost many of its men to the war effort.

There were other problems, however: in 1940 the whole country was in the grip of one of the worst winters in memory, with heavy snowfalls and deep drifts which closed roads and railways and cut communications for several days. Bolton did not escape this onslaught, and the snow clearers would have seen plenty of action for in just one weekend, 26th to 28th January 1940, twenty-three inches of snow fell.

Drifts of between 10 and 15ft accumulated and five trams were marooned on Bolton Road, Westhoughton near to the Snydale water tower. On the Monday some 1,657 extra men were taken on to help clear the snow and it was to take all week. Many trams were out of action due to snow damage in their motors. What a start to the new year.

Things eventually returned to what then passed for normality and it was then decided to renumber the surviving trams so as to avoid confusion with the ever-growing bus fleet. Accordingly, during 1940, all the trams had 300 added to their existing fleet numbers.

Aside from the daily pressures members of the MPTA were able to meet at St James's Church, Breightmet, in June 1940, to attend a service of Memorial and Dedication to the late John Barnard. The Memorial, the gift of his widow, took the form of a children's corner and stained

Tram number 330 about to cross Long Causeway, Farnworth, on a wartime journey to Walkden and displaying the letter **G**, previously used for **Great Lever** but used for **Walkden** when letters were reused during the war whilst destination names were not allowed to be displayed to confuse spies. The complexity of the overhead lines, with tram wires crossing trolleybus overhead, is quite remarkable with a huge weight of equipment in the air to separate the various positive and negative wires. *(66 Group)*

The winter snow storms of 26th to 28th January 1940 were particularly heavy, and here a tram, No.308 (previously No. 8), has become stuck on the Westhoughton route. The view has been taken looking towards Bolton, with Snydale Hill behind the photographer. In the background is the headgear for Deane Colliery, which was the last working pit in Bolton and is now the site of Barton Grange Garden Centre. The use of a four-wheel open-balcony car on the Westhoughton route was unusual by this time, and it is possible that No. 308 had been sent out as a snow plough and had itself got stuck. The story goes that when this picture appeared in the local press, one of the schoolboys to the left of the tram was in trouble for not having being in school at the time of the photograph. *(66 Group)*

glass window in one of the chapels. Mr Barnard had been a lifelong member of the Church and a Sunday school teacher there, a point made at his funeral back in August 1938. Dedicated by the Vicar, the window was unveiled by Mr GG Altham, Worshipful Master of the Boltonian Lodge of Freemasons, another organisation with which Mr Barnard had also long been associated.

In the years 1938 to 1942 Bolton Transport had taken delivery of four single-deck and 100 double-deck buses. Included in the double-deckers were ten with the first double-deck bodies to be built by East Lancashire Coachbuilders. Many of these vehicles had been intended for the planned replacement of trams whilst the remainder were for the replacement of time-served buses.

Due to the outbreak of war in 1939, the tram replacement programme had to be deferred. Indeed there was a renaissance of sorts when the 78 remaining cars, working the surviving five routes, carried more passengers than ever due to buses having to be taken off through fuel shortages.

This deferment, together with the fact that the older buses intended for replacement were still serviceable, had a twofold effect. On the one hand it meant that Bolton did not need to purchase any complete new buses to the wartime specification, whilst on the other hand it meant that Bolton was in a position to hire vehicles to other operators who were in need of them and, because of wartime restrictions, were unable to purchase sufficient new vehicles to meet their requirements. This programme of hirings was quite extensive and details of the vehicles involved and the operators to whom they were hired, together with dates of hiring, are given in the relevant Appendix.

Although there was a surplus of vehicles, this situation did not apply to staff, with many

BOLTON CORPORATION TRANSPORT.

HALLIWELL ROUTE.

TRAMCAR SERVICE
COMMENCING MONDAY, 1st APRIL, 1940.

TIME TABLE.

MONDAY TO FRIDAY		SATURDAY		SUNDAYS	
OUTWARD	INWARD	OUT	IN	OUTWARD	IN
5 21 8 51 12 22 2 44	5 39 9 9 12 40 3 2 6 38			8 50 7 41	9 10 7 34
5 39 9 0 12 27 2 51	5 57 9 17 12 45 3 9 6 42			9 10 7 48	9 30 7 43
5 57 9 9 12 31 2 58	6 15 9 26 12 49 3 16 6 46			9 28 7 53	9 50 7 51
6 15 9 17 12 36 3 5	6 33 9 34 12 54 3 23 6 49			9 48 8 0	10 10 7 58
6 21 9 26 12 40 3 12	6 39 9 43 12 58 3 30 6 54			10 8	10 30 8 5
6 27 9 34 12 45 3 19	6 45 9 51 1 3 3 37 6 58			10 28 and	10 50 8 11
6 33 9 43 12 49 3 26	6 51 10 0 1 7 3 44 7 1			10 48 every	11 10 8 18
5 39 9 51 12 54 3 33 11 0	6 57 10 9 1 12 3 51 7 6			11 8 7	11 30 8 25
6 45 10 0 12 58 3 40 11 7	7 3 10 17 1 16 3 58 7 10	11 43 11 43	11 28 min.	11 50 8 32
6 51 10 9 1 3 3 47 11 15	7 9 10 26 1 21 4 5 7 13	11 47 11 54	11 48 to	12 10
6 57 10 17 1 7 3 54	7 15 10 34 1 25 4 12 7 18	11 52 12 0	11 8	12 30 and
7 3 10 26 1 12 4 2	7 21 10 43 1 30 4 19 7 24	11 57 12 5	11 28 11 2	12 50 every
7 9 10 34 1 16 4 9	7 27 10 51 1 34 4 27 7 30	12 2 12 10	11 48 11 9	1 9 7
7 15 10 43 1 21 4 16	7 33 11 0 1 39 4 34			1 8 11 17	1 26 min.
7 21 10 51 1 25 4 20	7 39 11 9 1 43 4 38			1 26 11 25	1 43 to
7 27 11 0 1 30	7 45 11 17 1 47 4 42			1 43	2 0
7 33 11 9 1 34	7 51 11 26 1 52 4 46				11 20
7 39 11 17 1 39	7 57 11 34 1 57 4 50			and and	11 27
7 45 11 26 1 48	8 3 11 43 2 1 4 54			every every	11 35
7 51 11 34 1 48	8 9 11 52 2 6 4 58			8¼ 8¼	11 43
7 57 11 43 1 52	8 15 12 0 2 11 5 2	11 12 11 30	min. mins.	
8 3 11 47 1 57	8 21 12 5 2 15 5 6 11 0	11 18 11 36	to to	
8 9 11 51 2 0	8 27 12 9 2 19 11 6	11 24 11 42		
8 15 11 55 2 4 7 0	8 33 12 13 2 23 11 12	11 30 11 48	7 0	
8 21 12 0 2 9 7 6	8 39 12 18 2 27 11 18		7 5	7 0
8 27 12 5 2 16 7 12	8 44 12 22 2 34 11 26		7 9	7 9
8 33 1¼ 9 2 23 7 18	8 51 12 27 2 41 11 34		7 17	7 17
8 39 12 13 2 30 7 24	8 57 12 31 2 48 6 30		7 26	7 23
8 45 12 18 2 37 7 30	9 3 12 36 2 55 6 31		7 34	7 29

STAGES and FARES.

Stage No. 1		Trinity Church
3	—	Kay Street
4	1d. —	Eskrick Street
5	1½d. 1d. —	Halliwell Terminus

Timetable for the Halliwell route; what it doesn't make clear is that this was a *re-instatement* of the tram service. Trams had been replaced by buses in 1939, but due to wartime pressures on the fleet the trams were reinstated as shown. *(66 Group)*

This spectacular accident occurred on Wednesday 12th February 1941 when two cars collided on Folds Road with the result being seen only too clearly. Number 420, on its side, had run away and collided with the other car which was waiting in the loop for 420 to pass. The unfortunate car was further badly damaged by hitting the traction pole – fortunately it didn't bring it down.

Despite such extensive damage none of the 31 people involved was badly injured, and such was the need for operational trams that 420 was quickly repaired and put back into service. *(66 Group)*

76

members having been called to the armed forces as mentioned. Mr Jackson did not want to employ females and suggested the use of temporary male conductors of 18 years of age who could serve in this capacity for three years before being called up to the armed forces at 21 years of age.

This did not meet with the approval of the Town Clerk and, by 4th March 1940, female conductors were employed, one having worked in that capacity during World War 1. By 1947 over 650 females had been employed, the highest number at any time being 267. The suggestion that female drivers be employed did not materialise.

Bolton had always been fortunate that its trams had not been involved in any serious accidents until, in 1941, in circumstances not now recorded, two cars collided, resulting in one turning over onto its side in the street. There were no serious injuries, and, because of the need for every available tram to be pressed into service, the badly damaged No. 420 was rebuilt to see another day.

An unusual situation was the employment from December 1941 of male auxiliary conductors who travelled free to and from work in the ratio of one per bus. They were provided with identity cards plus armlets with blue and gold lettering to be worn whilst on duty and by January 1942 their number reached 80.

Local enthusiasts were also able to take part in the war effort – Alan Ralphs, whose father was a tram driver, Derek Shepherd, and the late Gwynne Thomas all had tales to tell in later years. Alan became a 'helper' by moving trams around the depot as a semi-official shunter, and also recovered demic cars which had become stranded with faults. This experience stood him in good stead when he joined Metro-Vick in Trafford Park, eventually becoming one of their traction control specialists.

Derek also assisted in many ways and after the war became an employee of the Electricity Department, later the CEGB, and was eventually responsible for decommissioning Kearsley Power Station, one of the former Lancashire Electric Power Company's stations.

Whilst supervising the run-down at Back o'th Bank generating station (which had replaced Spa Road in 1914) after its working days were over, he put his time and their facilities to good use, and completed and commissioned his own project, tramcar Bolton 66 which now operates in Blackpool. Later, at Kearsley, he assisted in converting two former Oporto coal trams into components for restored British trams.

Gwynne lived in Walkden, used the tram to get to school each day, and became a high-flier in pharmaceuticals. The tale is still told of his summons to Bolton School's head one morning after assembly. "If you must drive those dreadful trams on your way into school Thomas, at least take your school cap off" he was admonished! Not all the auxiliaries wore arm bands . . .

Another wartime event was the change from Bell Punch tickets to TIM machines which printed ticket details on blank white rolls and 50 such machines were ordered on 26th November 1941 at a cost of £17 11s 6d each including cancellation punch. Bell Punch tickets were retained for joint services to meet the accounting requirements.

In order to conserve fuel, bus operators were directed to convert at least 10% of their fleet for Gas Production Unit operation. Bolton purchased 16 gas trailers at a cost of £1,893 0s 3d. It is not known how many vehicles were converted apart from No. 149, but the units were not popular with operators and it seems likely that many trailers were unused. In 1944 the Order was withdrawn and the trailers sold for £90. National negotiations then began to try to get a better than normal tax credit for machines which had never been used, but the Government was having none of it.

Although no complete new vehicles were purchased between 1942 and 1946 a programme of rebodying of existing vehicles was undertaken commencing in 1944. Included in this rebodying programme were the three Massey single-deck buses numbered 97-9 which received double-deck bodies and were renumbered 243-5. The rebodying was undertaken by two coachbuilding organisations which had been appointed by the Ministry of War Transport to undertake such work. One of these was Northern Coachbuilders of Newcastle upon Tyne which built bodies to the standard wartime specification. The other was East Lancashire Coachbuilders of Blackburn which continued to produce bus bodies very similar in outline to its pre-war products. How they managed to do this, when other coachbuilders had to build to the Ministry Standard Specification, remains something of a mystery. No satisfactory explanation to this was unearthed when the author wrote a book on the history of the company.

During the war, Bolton, like other operators, was obliged to convert 10% of its bus fleet to utilise other than liquid fuel, and one of ten producer gas trailers purchased in this connection is seen here. They only lasted two or three years and had to be stoked at each terminus to produce the gas which was fed by pipe under the bus to the engine. They reduced the engine's output, and were normally attached to petrol-engined vehicles. They were known to crews, who are seen here having the equipment demonstrated, as 'spud-roasters'. The staff are obviously bus drivers, as they are wearing soft-topped caps and have tunic jackets with lapels; at this time tram drivers were still issued with button-up tunics, doubtless very necessary when working on open-front trams during the winter. *(STA)*

Tram number 409 is seen during the war with headlamp masks and white painted fenders, while the rocker-panels are plain cream with the Bolton Corporation identification deleted. It is on the Black Horse route to Farnworth. This service was usually operated by the six ex-SLT trams acquired from Farnworth Council, but in the rush-hour other types were utilised to cope with the heavy demand, well demonstrated here on a tram which is packed to the gunnels. As up to 100 passengers could be crammed on, two conductors were required; one to collect the penny fares and one to give the bell signals and hold the trolley rope at junctions. Behind the tram is the building intended to be the Technical College which was finished just prior to the outbreak of war, but which was requisitioned by the RAF as a training school for the then new-fangled radar. It was not until after the war the local authority was able to use it for its original purpose. *(ADP)*

Adverts for Bell Punch and TIM ticket machines. Bell Punch pre-printed tickets were cancelled by the conductor using a punch built into his machine which emitted a sharp ping and alerted the passenger to the fact that his fare had been recorded. It punched a hole through the ticket, denoting the stage from which it was valid, and the small circular disc was held within the unit. These tiny discs were checked by teams of female scrutineers in cases where the amount paid in and the tickets remaining unsold did not tally. The TIM system, which was introduced in Bolton from 1940 to replace the Bell Punch system was a miniature printing machine which printed the ticket onto a plain white paper roll. The blank rolls had no value and the machine had its own recording and counting system to ease checking and reduce fraud. Initially used on trams, their use was subsequently extended to the motorbuses.
(STA both)

Another view as that of car 409, opposite, but now showing one of the ex-SLT cars which were the resident trams for the Farnworth route. There were only six, and eight cars were needed for the rush-hour service, hence the use of 409 and others when required. This tram is clearly full to bursting on its way to Farnworth from Bolton. These were powerful cars still with a good turn of speed even when carrying over 100 passengers as they regularly would do. *(ADP)*

BOLTON CORPORATION TRANSPORT

CHRISTMAS DAY

1944

The SUNDAY SERVICE OF TRAMCARS will be in operation between the following times :-

CHORLEY NEW ROAD

To Horwich - -	First Car 10-0 a.m.	Last Car 10-30 p.m.
From Horwich -	,, 10-10, 10-40 a.m.	,, 10-43 p.m.
From Lostock -	,, 10-22, 10-52 a.m.	,, 10-57 p.m.
From Albert Road -	,, 10-30, 11-0 a.m.	,, 11-5 p.m.

HALLIWELL

To Halliwell -	First Car 10-8 a.m.	Last Car 10-30 p.m.
From Halliwell -	,, 10-30 a.m.	,, 10-48 p.m.

TONGE MOOR

To Tonge Moor -	First Car 10-6 a.m.	Last Car 10-30 p.m.
From Tonge Moor -	,, 10-28 a.m.	,, 10-50 p.m.

WESTHOUGHTON

To Punch Lane -	First Car 10-10 a.m.	Last Car 10-30 p.m.
To Westhoughton	,, 12-23 p.m.	,, 10-20 p.m.
From Westhoughton	,, 12-49 p.m.	,, 10-52 p.m.
From Punch Lane -	,, 10-30 a.m.	,, 11-4 p.m.
From Hulton Lane, Deane	,, 10-35 a.m.	,, 11-11 p.m.

TROLLEY BUSES

The Sunday service of TROLLEY 'BUSES between Bolton and Leigh will be in operation, from 10-3 a.m.

Last Trolley Bus: 10-0 p.m. to LEIGH. 10-30 p.m. to ATHERTON

Transport Offices,
 BOLTON,
18th December, 1944.

A. A. JACKSON,
General Manager and Engineer.

P. & S.—C6359

Traffic Notice as displayed in the tramcars and buses for Christmas 1944. *(66 Group)*

In 1938 the Bolton Evening News captured a typical wet Saturday evening view in Deansgate. The bright lights would disappear just over a year later with the outbreak of war. *(66 Group)*

Bolton 451 was formerly Bury 55, purchased with two others bogie double-deckers in 1943 to ease the shortage of trams. It is seen at the start of Chorley New Road on a short working to Albert Road on the Horwich route in the summer of 1945, by which time the headlamp masking had been removed as hostilities eased. Its somewhat lethargic nature had been cured in Bolton by the substitution of a pair of bogies from one of the two scrapped SLT cars as recorded earlier. *(NTM)*

Post-War Developments

In 1946, as the bus fleet increased in size and the tram fleet declined as it approached its end, the availability of men and materials allowed Shiffnall Street Depot to be modified to accommodate buses, and alterations were commenced at Carlton Street Works to provide for the overhaul of buses. Very clearly the days of the trams were numbered now.

At the end of the war, the department had implemented a major fleet renewal programme. In 1946 a fleet of 75 new Crossley DD42/3 double-deckers arrived, intended for the tramway replacement scheme, and introducing a new livery.

Crossley at this time was still an independent manufacturer of commercial vehicles – the days of luxury car building had long gone – principally buses and trolleybuses, and was based in Stockport. Its coachwork was well-respected, its chassis perhaps less so. In 1948 it lost its independence when it was taken over to become part of the then new ACV empire, which consisted of AEC, Maudslay and Crossley. Chassis manufacture ceased in 1951, bodybuilding in 1958. In latter years BUT trolleybus chassis were assembled in the Errwood Park factory, including those for neighbouring Manchester Corporation.

The first 67 Crossleys had bodies by Sheffield-based Cravens, best described as 'semi-utility' with rather angular fronts but nevertheless well proportioned vehicles. The remaining eight had decidedly more handsome bodies by Crossley which were to the pre-war outline incorporating the curved waistlines associated for many years with buses of Manchester Corporation Transport.

Cravens were part of the giant John Brown organisation, builders of the Cunard liners Queen Mary and Queen Elizabeth, with steel manufacture at the heart of their business. Railway carriage builders from the 19th Century, they subsequently added tramcar and later bus building to their portfolio, and although they were not in the major bus building league they had supplied Stockport with some bus bodies in the 'thirties.

Both Cravens and Crossley were at full stretch in 1946, building vehicles for overseas in the 'Export or Die' push to raise desperately needed money to pay for imports of food and raw materials, and to start to pay off debts from the recent War.

The choice of chassis was something of a departure for Bolton from the pre-war standard choice of Leyland as chassis manufacturer. Leyland Motors, however, were also building large numbers of vehicles for export, and Government permits were required at this time by all manufacturers before materials – which were often not available – could even be ordered. Giants such as AEC and Leyland were now seen as the Country's salvation, and their export business took preference over almost everything else for many months. Private car production was even more strongly directed to export.

Cravens, eventually part of the mighty John Brown shipbuilding group, and based in Sheffield, were long-established as builders of railway carriages and tramcars, with buses being only a small percentage of their output. The order to body Bolton's large fleet of Crossleys must have been received with some relief in the difficult immediate post-war period. Neepsend and East Lancashire Coachbuilders would, in due course, become part of the group, forming uncomfortable bed-fellows according to former ELCB management. *(STA)*

ii   PASSENGER TRANSPORT   April 9th 1948

BUSES · TROLLEY BUSES · COACHES

ALL METAL OR
COMPOSITE
CONSTRUCTION

CRAVENS
BODY BUILDERS. SHEFFIELD

Telephones
Attercliffe 41391 (4 lines)
London , Abbey 6055

Telegrams
Craven, Sheffield
Craonoff, Parl, London

London Office -
8, The Sanctuary,
Westminster. S.W. 1

Bolton had a number of reconditioned chassis fitted with new bodies during the war, these being supplied by either Northern Coachbuilders of Newcastle-upon-Tyne or East Lancashire Coachbuilders of Blackburn. In the post-war period some of these bodies were transferred to chassis from later (pre-war) chassis. Whilst the ELCB contract ran smoothly, problems were encountered with the NCB contract with regard to delays, a problem which had also been experienced with this coachbuilder by Cumberland in their wartime and post-war contracts. This NCB body dating from 1945 was originally fitted to Leyland TD4c No. 19, and was transferred to this vehicle – No. 207 – in 1949. It is parked alongside two of the 1946 Cravens-bodied Crossleys, Nos. 309 and 247, together with a selection of other vehicles. (AEJ)

Above: Number 166 from the 1939 delivery of Massey-bodied Leyland TD5c models was still looking quite smart when photographed 10 years later in September 1949, alongside a recently delivered Leyland-bodied Leyland PD2 No.416. *(RM)*

Centre: Number 193, AWH 931, was numerically the first of the 1940 batch of Massey-bodied Leyland Titan TD5c models. It is shown here in April 1949 parked in Bolton having returned on service 23. Note the then typical situation of a small shop located in the row of terraced houses in the background. *(RM)*

Below: The last 25 of the 50 Leyland TD5c models ordered for delivery during 1940/1 were built to the recently introduced TD7c specification; they included number 227 shown parked in Bolton in June 1951. *(RM)*

A number of the 1940-2 Massey Bodied Leyland TD5c and TD7c s were rebodied with second hand bodies removed from older chassis but No. 213 dating from 1941 still retained its original body when photographed at Moor Lane in November 1957. The flush rubber mounted perimeter glazing which is evident in this view indicates that some rebuilding of the body had taken place. Also the original outswept lower panels had been replaced. The lower edge of the number X66 is just visible in the service number display. Reference to the inclusion of this number is made in the text. (KWS)

The first example of the Cravens-bodied Crossley DD42/3 models, Number 248, still in grey primer before the Bolton post-war colour scheme had been finalised, awaits application of the Bolton post-war colour scheme. It is shown undergoing tilt testing at Cravens Sheffield works.

The first new vehicles to arrive after the war were 67 Crossley DD42/3 models with bodywork by Cravens of Sheffield. Bolton would have preferred Leylands but the order for chassis and bodies was placed at the directive of the Ministry. Delivery commenced in 1946 and was completed in April 1947. The body design with its angular appearance was reminiscent of wartime designs although Cravens never built any bodies to the wartime specification... They were however well-proportioned and to some eyes quite attractve vehicles and, most importantly, gave good service. The standard Crossley arrangement of low slung engine and radiator allowed a deep windscreen to be fitted and this aided driver visibility. Some of them remained in service until 1962. The final colour scheme is seen on the finished vehicle on the facing page. (STA both)

In 1950 No. 198 dating from 1940 had its Massey body replaced by this East Lancashire Coachbuilders 'Wartime' example dating from 1945 and previously fitted to number 38. Northern Coachbuilders built strictly to the Ministry of Supply Wartime Standard Specification with very angular lines as the photographs show. As explained in the text, East Lancashire Coachbuilders managed to produce bodies to what was basically their standard pre-war design. (KWS)

Farewell to the Trams

With the receipt of new buses the plan to abandon the tramway was revived, with the intention to have it completed in 1947, and work to this end moved quickly with routes being closed as follows :–

Nov. 1944 :-	Moses Gate to Black Horse and Walkden (former SLT)
Aug. 1945 :-	Halliwell (for second time)
Oct. 1946 :-	Horwich (incl. shed closure)
Nov. 1946 :-	Westhoughton
Dec. 1946 :-	Deane
Mar. 1947 :-	Tonge Moor

The long route to Horwich had been earmarked as the last to be closed, but the state of the roadway and its effect on the track dictated otherwise. The shed, which also closed when the route was converted to bus operation in 1946, still stands with its proud inscription above the doorways.

The following year, 1947, started off in chaos throughout Britain. Many miners were unhappy about some aspects of the newly-formed National Coal Board, and absenteeism after the New Year break reached record levels. This hit coal exports hard, and then came a return of the terrible winter conditions of 1940, but this time even worse.

Once again transport and communications throughout the country were brought to a standstill through blizzards which left deep snowdrifts for mile after mile along the roads. One stretch of the Great North Road was closed for 22 miles with 10ft deep snowdrifts. Five hundred prisoners were brought out from jail to assist with snow clearing in Yorkshire.

With coal trains trapped in drifts up to 20ft deep in places, power stations were now starved of coal and electricity was only available for short periods each day. And the misery was not confined to land transport; fishing fleets were unable to put to sea and supplies of fish were soon exhausted in the days before many people had refrigerators.

Those responsible for clearing these drifts in Bolton would have been glad of the snow-broom – sadly it had been scrapped with the other two works cars as the end of the trams approached in the late 'thirties, and space was at a premium as Bridgeman Street depot was converted from tram to bus accommodation. Spades were trumps . . .

At that time it would have seemed a reasonable risk, since the tram's days were numbered and there hadn't been a really bad winter for some years. The best laid plans . . . ?

A scene in Trinity Street after turning the corner from Newport Street where the leading tram is ready to set out for Halliwell. The rear tram will be going to Tonge Moor and is No. 420, seen earlier in 1941 on page 76 overturned on its side. It was completely rebuilt following the accident. *(ADP)*

As the worst of the weather subsided it was time to say farewell to the trams and, in accord with tradition, car 440 was decorated and fitted with illuminated displays, running to Tonge Moor to let everyone see it and a lucky few have the chance for a last nostalgic ride. The last service car was number 406, chosen as having been the last new car to enter the fleet and thus being the youngest. It was specially cleaned by the local enthusiasts for its final duty on Saturday night, 29th March.

Official figures published after the closure recorded that between 1900 and 1947 the electric trams had carried 1,750 million passengers, paid almost £260,000 into rate relief, and that the peak year had been 1928/9 when approximately 60 million had been carried.

Bolton was not the only system to close at the end of March 1947, and it was not alone in being short of buses to complete the changeover. Neighbour Charles Baroth was on a real cliff-hanger, for the buses he needed to complete his conversion in Salford were actually delivered on the morning of Monday 31st March enabling the trams to be withdrawn that evening. Tramway enthusiasts had a busy time that weekend; after the Saturday night closure in Bolton there was a tour on Pilcher tram 502 on the Sunday in Manchester, and then the end of Salford's trams on the Monday. It brought home the fact that soon

other systems would close and the great north west tramway empire would be no more.

Whereas Salford's trams were broken up at Manchester's Hyde Road permanent way yard, Bolton's were broken up at their own depot.

Nearly 60 years after the closure, restored tram 66 was being prepared for another season's service (including the famous illuminations) in Blackpool, and thoughts turned to how it might be decorated to celebrate its own centenary. The idea was floated of having something similar to the star used on that last decorated car in Bolton, but what had been the colour scheme? Even Derek Shepherd, guru of matters tramway Boltonian, was more than a little surprised when his friend Alan Ralphs produced the original assembly from his loft to enable the details to be obtained.

A colour illustration of 66, specially decorated for its own centenary, appears at the end of this book giving a taste of how things looked on that last night all those years ago.

Car 450 was numerically the highest numbered car in the original Bolton fleet, having been numbered 150 when delivered in 1927. It was the success of these totally enclosed cars which led the department to begin to enclose the top decks of its balcony cars, though in fact only about half were so treated. Down below, the driver was left out in the cold, for to enclose the platform would have involved major work on the brake rigging, brake handle and controller positions. *(66 Group)*

Closing Dates – Electric Trams

Victoria Road and Lee Lane, Horwich	31st December 1907
Darcy Lever	10th March 1928
Church Road	28th February 1933
Breightmet & Bury	21st January 1934
Four Lane Ends	28th March 1936
Great Lever	30th April 1936
Swan Lane	16th August 1936
Dunscar	3rd October 1937
Montserrat	31st December 1938
Halliwell	13th August 1939
(Reopened	1st April 1940)
Black Horse	12th November 1944
Walkden	12th November 1944
Moses Gate (Sunday mornings & Football Specials)	May 1946
Halliwell	5th August 1945
Horwich	6th October 1946
Westhoughton	3rd November 1946
Deane	11th December 1946
Tonge Moor	29th March 1947

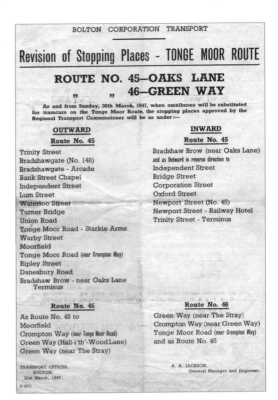

Illuminated car number 440, seen standing in the side street alongside the depot, was to make the final ceremonial journey at 11.30pm on 29th March 1947. This car had been chosen since by then it had only one good motor, too slow for being used in service, but making it ideal for running slowly through the streets and allowing everyone to see it. *(66 Group)*

BOLTON CORPORATION TRANSPORT

Revision of Stopping Places - TONGE MOOR ROUTE

ROUTE NO. 45—OAKS LANE
"   "   46—GREEN WAY

As and from Sunday, 30th March, 1947, when omnibuses will be substituted for tramcars on the Tonge Moor Route, the stopping places approved by the Regional Transport Commissioner will be as under :—

OUTWARD — Route No. 45

Trinity Street
Bradshawgate (No. 148)
Bradshawgate - Arcade
Bank Street Chapel
Independent Street
Lum Street
Waterloo Street
Turner Bridge
Union Road
Tonge Moor Road - Starkie Arms
Warby Street
Moorfield
Tonge Moor Road (near Crompton Way)
Ripley Street
Danesbury Road
Bradshaw Brow - near Oaks Lane Terminus

INWARD — Route No. 45

Bradshaw Brow (near Oaks Lane) and as Outward in reverse direction to
Independent Street
Bridge Street
Corporation Street
Oxford Street
Newport Street (No. 45)
Newport Street - Railway Hotel
Trinity Street - Terminus

Route No. 46

As Route No. 45 to
Moorfield
Crompton Way (near Tonge Moor Road)
Green Way (Hall-i'th'-Wood Lane)
Green Way (near The Stray)

Route No. 46

Green Way (near The Stray)
Crompton Way (near Green Way)
Tonge Moor Road (near Crompton Way)
and as Route No. 45

TRANSPORT OFFICES,
BOLTON.
21st March, 1947.
D 2711.

A. A. JACKSON,
General Manager and Engineer.

The End – buses are to replace Bolton's last trams. *(66 Group)*

Buses Reign Supreme

After the sadness at the passing of an era thoughts turned, naturally, to the future. Whilst the trams had given good service they had become run down in later years, and thus a brighter note was provided by an influx of shiny new buses, smelling of new paint and upholstery. These marked a return to Leyland as supplier with the arrival of 30 Leyland PD1 chassis, the initial 15 having bodies by Northern Counties Motor and Engineering Company of Wigan, the first buses supplied by this builder to Bolton, and the remaining 15 by Crossley. The intake of new vehicles continued in 1948 with the arrival of the first 8ft wide and the first air-braked buses – 50 Leyland PD2/4s, with Leyland bodies, followed by a further 50 in 1949. Those delivered in 1949 incorporated a revised front destination display layout with a three track service number facility centrally placed above the destination aperture. Also delivered in 1949 were three Crossley SD42/7 single-deckers with Crossley bodies. Not surprisingly the 100 Leyland bodied PD2/4 buses seemed to dominate the Bolton bus scene for many years. The PD2/4 variety of the PD2 model was provided with air brakes and the only operators to take delivery were Bolton and Bury.

At the time these buses were delivered, Coras Iompair Eireann, the major bus operator in Southern Ireland, were in need of a large quantity of double-deckers and whereas they had previously built their own bodies, their works could not cope with demand at this time. As a result of this, they purchased 100 PD2/3 chassis fitted with Leyland bodies to the Bolton specification, even to the extent of using the Bolton destination display arrangement of the type provided on the first Bolton batch.

In June 1949 the title of the undertaking was altered – somewhat belatedly – from Tramways to Transport Department, again reflecting the demise of the trams. Many other undertakings had taken this step early in the 'thirties when buses were becoming the growth area of more modern transport within the organisation. Another move bringing the department more up-to-date saw a sprinkler system installed in each of the depots.

A return to Leyland Motors as supplier was made in 1947, with the purchase of 30 PD1 models, 15 of which had bodies by Northern Counties Motor & Engineering Company Limited of Wigan. These were the only bodies supplied by this firm to Bolton, and No. 334 was photographed when new in these three views by the coachbuilders (below, facing and overleaf) in the location regularly used by them. The treatment of the front domes would later create a design every bit as distinctive as Massey's curvature would become. The broadside views show a well-balanced and pleasing design which would appear in many fleets and on a variety of chassis makes. *(STA all)*

The last eight of the 1946 Crossley DD42/3 double-deckers were provided with Crossley bodies. These were to the design introduced by Crossley to the requirements of Manchester Corporation Transport with curved waistrails at the front and raised waistrails at the rearmost side windows where the upper-deck framing was supporting the cantilevered back platform. They were in sharp contrast to the angular design of the Cravens bodies, an example of which is visible at the rear. *(STA)*

Flanked on both sides by Leyland bodied PD2s No. 318, another Crossley-bodied Crossley, stands in Howell Croft Bus Station. The frontal appearance of these vehicles was marred by the old-fashioned looking deep mudguards as can be seen when comparing the same body on Leyland chassis on page 96. *(HPC)*

In this post-1949 scene another of the 1946 Cravens-bodied Crossleys, No. 291, turns from Newport Street, Bolton followed by one of the undeniably more handsome 1949 Leyland-bodied Leyland PD2s. *(HPC)*

An offside view of Cravens-bodied Crossley No. 302, parked in Victoria Square in front of the War Memorial in September 1949, confirms that they did not really have a 'best side'! *(RM)*

Parked outside the well-known Bolton engineering firm of Hick Hargreaves and Company Limited is No. 200, dating from 1941 but fitted in 1949 with the Northern Coachbuilders body removed from No 84. This body had been built to the 'Relaxed Utility Specification' in late 1945, being relicensed in January 1946 *(RM)*

Another reminder of wartime is provided by No. 83, a 1934 Leyland TD3c with Bromilow & Edwards body photographed at Golders Green whilst on hire to London Transport. A plaque on display in the Greater Manchester Museum of Transport at Boyle Street carries the small plates affixed to the front bulkhead on all the Bolton buses loaned to LPTB, recording for posterity the part they played in helping out in the Capital's time of need. *(RMC)*

The balance of the 15 Leyland PD1 models were fitted with bodies by Crossley Motors of Stockport, generally to the same design as the bodies supplied by this firm the previous year on Crossley chassis. Number 349 was photographed in Howell Croft Bus Station during October 1953. The ledge below the windscreen indicates that Crossley had utilised the cab front supplied by Leyland Motors as part of the chassis fittings. *(KWS)*

The nearside view of the Crossley body confirms the smooth lines typical of most good coachbuilders in those halcyon days. Number 350, numerically the last of the batch, was caught in this view at the Leigh terminus of service 16 from Horwich. *(STA)*

In 1948 No. 214 received the 1945 wartime Northern Coachbuilders body from 1936-built Leyland TD4 No. 17 and is shown with this latter body in August 1949, heading for Church Road on service 1. *(RM)*

Another example of an East Lancashire Coachbuilders body supplied in wartime is shown fitted to No. 202, dating from 1941. The body, which was supplied in 1945, was originally fitted to 1936 Leyland TD4c No. 34. *(RM)*

This view taken in October 1953 shows 1938 Leyland TD5c No.148 looking very smart having been rebodied with the 1945 'Relaxed Utility' Northern Coachbuilders body from No. 85. By this time the body had been the subject of rebuilding, including the provision of flush mounted perimeter glazing as can be seen. *(AEJ)*

Northern Coachbuilders were gearing up for expansion after the war, and recruited Bill Bramham to join them in their new factory in Team Valley in June 1948. Seconded to the Government for the war effort, Bramham had been in charge at Eastern Coach Works, and previously with CH Roe in Leeds. SN Churchill was also at NCB, having been at Brush and then Chas Roberts. By 1951, things were unsettled and so both men left, Bramham joining East Lancashire Coachbuilders as a technical representative. *(STA)*

The post-war style of Northern Coachbuilders body was subjected to rebuilding in Bolton as shown by No. 203 carrying the 1946 body previously fitted to No. 24. *(RM)*

The 1946 Northern Coachbuilders style of post-war body design is illustrated in this view of No. 212, photographed in June 1951. The body had originally been fitted to 1933 Leyland TD3 No. 76 and was transferred to No. 212, which had previously carried a Massey body, in 1949 when only three years old. *(RM)*

Also in 1949 No. 211 received the 1946 post-war style of NCB body dating from 1946 previously fitted to 1934 Leyland TD3c No. 89. The front upper-deck windows provided an easy point of identity for NCB bodies – they were in a v format, set back at the outer edges of the body. *(RM)*

During 1948/9 Bolton purchased 100 Leyland PD2/4 models with Leyland bodywork, batches of 50 being supplied in each year. One hundred similar vehicles in a fleet the size of Bolton's meant that these buses seemed to dominate the Bolton scene for a number of years. Number 353 was one of the 1948 batch, and is shown in Trinity Street, approaching Holy Trinity Church. *(RM)*

Mr Ronald Edgely Cox joined the department in 1949 as Deputy General Manager but his stay at Bolton was short. Later in the year he moved to St Helens as General Manager and whilst there introduced new London Transport type AEC RT double-deckers, the only operator outside London to purchase new examples of this excellent vehicle. Three years later he moved to become General Manager of Walsall's undertaking.

The year 1949 had also seen the introduction of a radio control system to assist in the operation of services and then in April 1951 external advertising was re-introduced as a source of additional income but this was not without controversy. When it was first proposed, various councillors were opposed, not to the advertising, but as to what should be included. They considered football pools and drinks adverts to be unsuitable. Councillor Lucas wanted Bolton to be a beautiful and attractive town and did not want the town's buses to be 'mobile sandwich boards'. Councillor Vickers asked sardonically, why the town should not go

RE Cox, who joined the department in 1949

the whole hog and rent the front of the town hall and the mayoral car to an advertising agency. Correspondents to the local newspaper were split on the matter with reference being made to Ribble 'White Lady' double-deck coaches which did not carry adverts because, according to one councillor, they did not want to spoil the appearance of the vehicle, and they believed this should also apply in Bolton.

By 1952 the department was showing a deficit, and in that year, tours of Bolton were introduced to operate the second week of Bolton Holidays and in September. The tours were of two hours duration and included a 30 minute stop at either Smithills Hall, Hall i'th' Wood, Belmont, Affetside or Barrow Bridge, the cost being 2 shillings (10p) for adults and 1 shilling (5p) for children. At the end of 1952 the Council set up a special committee of councillors who were not on the Transport Committee, and Consultants were appointed to look at possible economies. The losses continued in 1953 and it was said that the Department was losing £1,000 per week, whilst the Consultants were being paid £500 per month for their investigations and preparation of the report. Services were cut and this led to letters to the local newspaper which included suggestions that the department should be sold to Ribble.

In August 1953, as part of the on-going drive to reduce operating costs, an Essex bus washing plant was installed in Bridgeman Street Garage. The Essex machine was suspended from the roof, and dropped down in a frame to wash the vehicle.

At this time of general decline in passenger numbers, which was not limited to Bolton, one aspect of the department's business was thriving. In 1953 agreement was reached with

The most noticeable difference between the two big batches of Leyland-bodied PD2/4 models was the arrangement of the front destination display. The single-line destination display with single-track service number blind alongside, which had been the Bolton standard arrangement for many years, was replaced by a single-line destination display with three-track service number display mounted above. Number 438 is at Lever Park awaiting return to Bolton. *(RM)*

Ribble to supply vehicles for the popular X60 service between Manchester and Blackpool and the peak was reached in 1955 with Bolton buses operating on Ribble's three Bolton to Blackpool services, X60, X90 and X100 and also on the X50 to Morecambe. Vehicles were used on the X9 Bury to Blackpool service with up to twelve double-deckers being so employed during Bury Wakes weeks, with most vehicles returning from Blackpool to Oldham. Bolton vehicles were also used on Webster's services from Bolton and St.Helens to North Wales.

Having purchased 208 new buses since 1946, the department was now well equipped with modern stock and no further purchases were made until 1955. However, whilst awaiting the arrival of these vehicles in 1955, it experienced a temporary shortage and this was resolved by hiring machines from other operators. This was of course a complete reversal of the situation in the

Whilst awaiting the arrival of new vehicles in 1955 Bolton experienced a vehicle shortage and vehicles were hired from other operators. Included amongst these from Warrington were above, No 85, BED 458, a 1937 Leyland-bodied Leyland TD5 which was withdrawn later in the year.

Here we see number 30, ED 8706, also from Warrington, a Metro-Cammell bodied Leyland TD3 dating from 1935 and which was withdrawn in 1955. The sharply raked windscreen does little for the appearance. *(AEJ both)*

Included in buses hired from Wallasey was No. 83, a 1946 Leyland PD1 with Metro-Cammell body in the very distinctive Wallasey livery officially described as 'Primrose Green and Cream'. The continued use of such large lettering, dating back to tramway days, was also noteworthy.

Local operator Ramsbottom Urban District Council provided two vehicles, numbered 23 and 25. These were 1947 Leyland PD2s with Leyland bodies and No. 25 is shown here. *(AEJ both)*

previous decade when Bolton was in a position to hire vehicles to others. The operators who assisted were Ramsbottom with their Nos. 23 and 25, Warrington with Nos. 30, 84 and 89, Wallasey with Nos. 83 and 88, and Wigan with Nos. 7, 10, 108, 112, 116 and 118.

Although Leyland bodywork predominated in the fleet at this time, Leyland had abruptly ceased the manufacture of bus bodies in 1953 and the department had therefore to look elsewhere for its requirements.

By 1955 the underfloor engined chassis had established itself as the standard single-deck format and Bolton received a Leyland Royal Tiger PSU1/14 with East Lancashire body. The double-deck requirement was fulfilled by 15 Leyland PD2/13 with bodies by Metropolitan Cammell Carriage and Wagon Company of Birmingham, and a Leyland PD2/12 with body by SH Bond of Wythenshawe, Manchester. These vehicles introduced a new style of destination display which was to continue until the arrival of the rear engined double-deckers in 1963. This display comprised, at the front, a rectangular aperture with a single line destination blind at the bottom and a three track service number system mounted centrally above. At the side there was a single line destination display and at the rear a three track service number display.

Opposite page: Having invested heavily in fleet renewal between 1946 and 1949 no further double-deckers were required until 1955 when fifteen Leyland PD2/13 with Metropolitan Cammell Weymann 'Orion' style bodies were purchased. Leyland had by this date ceased the manufacture of bus bodies. The 'Orion' was designed as a lightweight body in an attempt to conserve fuel. The traditional Bolton livery of maroon with three cream bands helped to alleviate the rather ungainly appearance brought about by the use of deep lower-saloon and shallow upper-saloon windows. They were numbered 51-65 and No. 60 was photographed when new. There were complaints about the ride quality of these buses, and Leyland fitted different rear springs to one bus which was demonstrated to the Transport Committee on 17th September 1956 and approved for fitment to the whole batch. *(STA)*

The first single-decker to be purchased since the Crossleys in 1949 was the Leyland PSU1/14 model with underfloor engine and with body by East Lancashire Coachbuilders seen opposite. It was numbered 9, and is shown leaving Moor Lane Bus Station for Affetside in November 1957. The small plates on the front panel and behind the door warn passengers to be ready to pay the driver on entry. Note the interesting selection of coaches in the background. *(KWS)*

Another view of No. 9, below, shows it this time in Blackburn bus station, awaiting time to return to Bolton on service 225 in July 1961. *(RM)*

SH Bond Ltd. of Wythenshawe, Manchester, was trying to break into the bus body building business at this time and had carried out some finishing work on three airport coaches built by HV Burlingham of Blackpool for Manchester Corporation. When East Lancashire Coachbuilders closed their Bridlington works, some rebuilding of wartime bodies for Coventry Corporation was diverted to Bonds. Work had also been undertaken for Ribble Motor Services on the rebuilding of wartime double-deck bodies and for South Lancashire Transport on the rebuilding of trolleybus bodies. The only other complete new bodies supplied were to Ashton-under-Lyne Corporation which received ten trolleybus bodies and four bodies on Guy Arab chassis. Some records suggest that they were built on frames supplied by Ashcroft Brothers of Birkenhead. However, this seems unlikely as in his book on Birkenhead Buses, TB Maund suggests that the Ashcroft bodies for Birkenhead, which were the only bodies supplied by Ashcroft, were built on Metal Sections frames. The likely explanation is that Ashcroft supplied the framework using Metal Sections components.

In 1956 Bonds provided a single-deck body on a Leyland PSU1/13 chassis for Bolton and this appears to have been the only single-deck body built by them. Bonds also supplied a further nine bodies on Leyland PD2/13 chassis but it has been stated that demarcation problems arose with trade unions and this led the firm to withdraw from the bus building business. The remainder of the 1956 delivery comprised nine Leyland PD2/13 chassis with bodies by Metro-Cammell.

An unusual vehicle for a municipal fleet was this Bedford SBQ with Duple luxury coach body, numbered 11, and supplied in 1956 as a 'Committee Coach'. It had limited usage and, being in good condition with low mileage, was soon sold in 1962 to Lightfoots of Widnes, later passing into Wales with Parrys of Lythfaen in 1965 before being scrapped in 1970. Salford were also firmly wedded to the concept of Committee Coaches, using a former Tognarelli vehicle, then a Burlingham-bodied Daimler and finally a Weymann Fanfare coach on an AEC Reliance chassis. When that vehicle passed to SELNEC it was swiftly put to work on a service to Manchester Airport – its accumulated mileage was extremely low and rumour has it that the spare wheel had never been out of its carrier. (KWS)

One other double-decker received in 1955 was this Leyland PD2/12 with body by SH Bond of Wythenshawe, Manchester. This firm was trying to break into the bus bodybuilding market, having carried out some finishing work and refurbishment work on other bodies. This example had been a demonstrator and was numbered 66 in the Bolton fleet. Douglas Bailey MBE, looking back to his time at Bolton, recalls this was his favourite bus. The chassis was an odd one out at Bolton, having vacuum brakes rather than air brakes on which Bolton standardised. It is shown in Leigh having worked on the 16 service from Horwich. *(RM)*

As far as can be ascertained, Bond built only one single-deck body complete, and this was supplied to Bolton in 1956 on a Leyland Royal Tiger PSU1/13 chassis and given fleet number 10. It is shown at Shiffnall Street Depot. *(RM)*

The year 1957 brought a surprise in that 21 Daimler CVG6K chassis were ordered, a make not previously ordered by Bolton. The reason for the change seems to have been that some members of the Transport Committee were not happy about all the business going to Leyland Motors. Did the earlier yardstick from the 'twenties and 'thirties of placing business locally to support local companies and keep employment secure in the area cut no ice with the Committee, or was it a ploy to try to keep Leyland Motors on its toes? The body contract was split between East Lancashire Coachbuilders which supplied ten and Metro-Cammell which supplied eleven. This was another significant point with regard to coachbuilders. East Lancashire had not supplied bodies on new double-deck chassis since 1938 when the first ten double-deckers which they built were supplied to Bolton, as previously mentioned. From this point onwards they were to figure prominently in orders for Bolton, eventually becoming the sole supplier.

In 1956 the maximum length for double-deckers on 2-axle chassis had been increased from 27ft 6ins to 30ft and Bolton took advantage of this for the 1958 deliveries. There were seven Daimlers with Metro-Cammell bodies and records suggest that the first of the Daimlers was the first 30ft-long 2-axle bus chassis produced by the company. The remainder of the 1958 delivery comprised ten Leyland PD3/5 chassis with East Lancashire Coachbuilders bodies.

The main talking point in 1958, however, was to do with the demise of the South Lancashire Transport Company's trolleybus system, and, perforce, Bolton's. The Leigh-Bolton route was one of the remaining two, and following closure on 31st August the 'Bolton Four' were unceremoniously delivered to Bridgeman Street bus depot pending disposal by their owners Bolton Corporation. They were sold to Birds of Stratford on Avon who scrapped them soon afterwards.

Bolton had finally broken the link which had seen electricity playing its part in the Borough's transport for almost 60 years.

Posed by the SLT company's power station complex and depot – now completely eradicated and a fading memory even for older enthusiasts – is Bolton's No. 49, looking smart when photographed c1955. No clue existed that the vehicle was not what it appeared to be, just another member of the SLT fleet, with legal lettering and other details apparently confirming it as an Atherton-owned unit. *(JAS)*

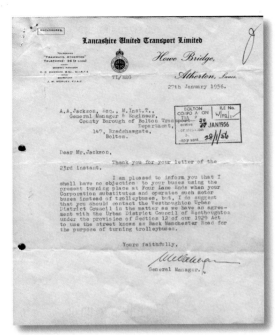

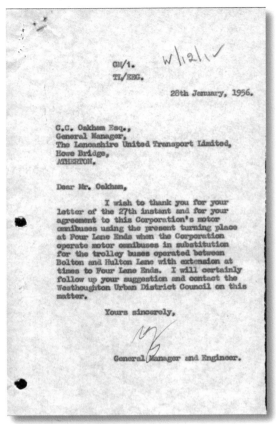

Amongst the minutia in the changeover from trolleybuses to motor buses, arrangements needed to be made for the buses to be able to continue to turn at Four Lane Ends and Mr Oakham, LUT's General Manager, was in touch with Mr Jackson at Bolton to make sure he was aware of the special provision that existed. *(STA courtesy GMTS)*

Shortly after the trolleybus service was withdrawn the four Bolton vehicles were returned to their rightful owners, and parked behind Bridgeman Street depot to await their fate. *(JAS)*

Bolton, obviously happy with the Bond body on the ex-demonstrator, purchased a further nine similar bodies on Leyland PD2/13 chassis in 1956. They were numbered 67-75 and the first of these is shown on Trinity Street, Bolton approaching Holy Trinity Church. The only other customer for Bond bodywork was Ashton under Lyne Corporation which received Bond bodies on both trolleybus and diesel bus chassis. *(RM)*

A nearside view of one of the Bond bodies supplied in 1956 is provided by No. 71 in Victoria Square, accompanied by a couple of cars from that era, the Morris Oxford on the right and the later Farina Oxford or Cambridge on the left. *(HPC)*

The other double-deck deliveries in 1956 were nine Metro-Cammell bodies, also on Leyland PD2/13 chassis, and numbered 76-84. The first of the batch was photographed before delivery from Birmingham when new. *(STA)*

In the mid-fifties, Ribble Motor Services went through a phase of linking services together and decided to link their service 347 from Chorley to Southport with their 122 service, which was operated jointly with Bolton, between Chorley and Bolton. As a result of this, Bolton's buses were to be seen in the villages of West Lancashire and also at the seaside in Southport. This through running commenced on 30th March 1957 and carried the service number 122.

Meanwhile back on the bus front, although the 1958 deliveries had all been 30ft long, the department still saw an application for the shorter vehicles and the 1959 delivery comprised five Leyland PD2/37 with Metro-Cammell bodies and five Leyland PD3/4 with East Lancashire bodies, these latter vehicles having front entrances, a feature which was new to Bolton but which was to become the standard for future deliveries.

Mr AA Jackson, who had been General Manager since coming from neighbouring St Helens in 1939, retired on 31st December 1959 thus completing 20 years service in post.

Facing page: 1957 saw a change of chassis supplier when the first Daimlers arrived and these carried the first East Lancashire Coachbuilders double-deck bodies to be supplied to Bolton since the rebodies of 1945. There were 21 in total, ten with ELCB bodies numbered 85-94 and eleven with MCW bodies numbered 95-105. The East Lancashire bodies had platform doors, a first for Bolton, and these are visible on No. 90 as it leaves Moor Lane Bus Station for Radcliffe on service 36 on 9th November 1956 against a background of buses and coaches – and the ever-present Town Hall Clock. *(KWS)*

An agreement had been reached with Ribble in April 1956 for through-running between Bolton and Southport. One of the East Lancashire-bodied Daimlers is shown in Southport Bus Station in March 1959. This fine terminal had originally been Lord Street Railway Station, and was converted into a bus station by Ribble in 1954 in the 'Hey Day of the Bus'. Sadly it was later claimed to be too elaborate and expensive to maintain, and was sold in 1987 by North Western who had taken over the southern area of Ribble. There is now a supermarket on the site. *(RM)*

115

Newport Street provides the setting for 1956 Daimler No. 99 with its Metro-Cammell bodywork and with the familiar outline of a Leyland-bodied PD2 behind. *(HPC)*

The 1958 Daimlers had a revised and more compact radiator grille and bonnet, often referred to as the 'Manchester' type, having been designed by Daimler in conjunction with Manchester Corporation Transport Department. Number 108 illustrates this in Victoria Square. This year was also notable for the arrival of the first 30ft-long double-deckers on 2 axles, following a relaxation of regulations, and this batch – which comprised Nos. 106-12 – were the first chassis Daimler manufactured to this revised length. *(HPC)*

Number 107 returned to the Daimler works in Coventry for a final checkover after bodying by Metro-Cammell and before delivery to the customer. *(STA)*

In the familiar surroundings of Moor Lane Bus Station, number 109 departs for Darcy Lever on service 14. The coach and private cars just visible beyond would also be worthy of attention nowadays. *(KWS)*

Leyland Motors also supplied 30ft long chassis in 1958, these being Titan PD3/5 models with bodies by East Lancashire Coachbuilders. Number 114 is shown above on 6th December 1958 at the Kay Gardens terminus in Bury, awaiting departure for return to Bolton on service 52. *(KWS)*

In a location regularly used for the photographing of new vehicles by East Lancashire Coachbuilders at Pleasington we see number 130, a Leyland PD3/4 in 1959, introducing another new feature to Bolton's double-deckers, that of a forward entrance with its large sliding door. *(STA)*

Later in the same day as the shot on the previous page the photographer, Ken Swallow, caught No. 114 again, this time leaving Bolton *en route* to Westhoughton on service 39. The large format camera has given us some excellent material for these illustrations. *(KWS)*

Diamond Jubilee Celebrations, and a Wind of Change arrives

On 1st January 1960 Ralph Bennett took up the post of General Manager to succeed Mr Jackson, having previously been General Manager at Great Yarmouth since 1958. His first introduction to Bolton was to oversee the already arranged Diamond Jubilee Exhibition held between 5th and 16th January 1960 at the Carlton Street Works. One member of staff is alleged to have said that "Mr Bennett swept through the department like a gale force wind".

Ralph Bennett had very definite ideas on vehicle design and presentation, ideas which were to have an impact on Bolton's buses for the remaining years of the Department's operation and also elsewhere as he moved on to Manchester. Initially, he introduced, for new vehicles, translucent fibreglass roof sections to double-deckers to create a brighter internal environment. He also introduced a new livery. The maroon with three cream bands, which had been in use since 1946 was replaced by cherry red with cream relief to the lower saloon window surrounds. This livery did, however, have a relatively short life, being replaced by the traditional maroon and cream but with greater areas of cream, the maroon being limited to the lower panels and roof.

A return to Daimler chassis was made in 1960 with the delivery of eight CVG6-30 models with East Lancashire bodies. The year 1961 saw a further new innovation for Bolton in that the ten Metro-Cammell bodies on Leyland PD2/27 chassis had full fronts as distinct from the traditional half-cabs but the eleven East Lancashire bodies on Leyland PD3/4 chassis retained the traditional half-cab style. A further surprise was the order for six AEC Regent V chassis, a make not previously specified by Bolton, and these were supplied with traditional half-cab bodies by Metro-Cammell.

The year 1962 saw the arrival of the first new single-decker since 1956 comprising a Leyland Leopard L2 chassis with body by East Lancashire. This body had been designed in close co-operation with Mr Bennett and was a sign of things to come. That year was also to see the end of the traditional front engined double-deckers as far as new deliveries were concerned although vehicles of this type, which had served the industry well for many years, were to continue to give excellent service. The final deliveries comprised nine Leyland PD3A/2 with East Lancashire bodies and eight similar chassis with Metro-Cammell bodies, all of full fronted design, a selection of which will be seen in the following pages.

It is certainly no exaggeration to say that Mr Bennett transformed not only Bolton's image, but to a very large extent that of the bus industry in general. New designs and attractive liveries made his vehicles stand out like beacons, and before long he was to move up the ladder to nearby Manchester – one of the topmost municipal managerial positions. He continued the good work there before moving to what might have been considered the number-one position in the country – the 'boss' at London Transport. Except, of course, that there was not one boss in London, but a host of politicians who by accident or design contrived to make the top job untenable. Ralph Bennett deserved better treatment than he got in the Capital, but we may be grateful that his finest hours were spent, arguably, in the north where his mark will ever be remembered. *(STA)*

COUNTY BOROUGH OF BOLTON

———

PROGRAMME

OF PROCEEDINGS IN CONNECTION

WITH THE CELEBRATION OF THE

Diamond Jubilee
of the
Transport Undertaking

1900 - 1960

———

4th JANUARY, 1960

COUNTY BOROUGH OF BOLTON

———

LUNCHEON

ON THE OCCASION OF THE

Diamond Jubilee
of the
Transport Undertaking

———

TOWN HALL, BOLTON

4th JANUARY, 1960

Reproductions of the covers of the two souvenir programmes produced in connection with the Diamond Jubilee of the Transport Undertaking, and the Order of Proceedings with the names of the officials. *(STA)*

TRANSPORT COMMITTEE

———

THE MAYOR
Alderman E. TAYLOR, J.P.

Chairman
ALDERMAN W. WALSH

Vice-Chairman
COUNCILLOR J. H. SMITH

Aldermen
W. BRADLEY, C.B.E., J.P.   H. WOOD

Councillors

T. S. BARLOW, J.P.	W. E. COCKBURN
C. S. BARNES	T. CONNOR, J.P.
A. BICKERSTAFFE	C. LEAT
J. BOOTHMAN	F. MAUGHAN
S. CHAMBERLAIN	H. G. SABINI
	A. TOWNEND

PHILIP S. RENNISON   R. F. BENNETT, A.I.MECH.E.
Town Clerk   *General Manager & Engineer*

ORDER OF PROCEEDINGS

———

a.m.

10.15   Assemble at Shiffnall Street Depot.

10.30   Inaugural ride, over the newly opened bus route to the Withins Estate via Deepdale Road, route No. 62.

11.0   Return to Carlton Street Overhaul Works for coffee.

11.15   Opening of the Transport Exhibition by His Worship the Mayor of Bolton, at the Carlton Street Overhaul Works.

p.m.

12.15   Assemble at Town Hall, Bolton, for Pre-Lunch Cocktails.

1.0   Luncheon.

The year 1959 also saw a return to 27ft long double-deckers with the purchase of five Leyland PD2/37 models with Metro-Cammell bodies. Number 125 illustrates this batch as it leaves Moor Lane Bus Station in April 1962. *(RM)*

Number 111 a 30ft-long Daimler CVG6 with Metro-Cammell body delivered in 1958 is shown in Bury awaiting return to its home town on service 52 in December 1958. *(KWS)*

The ten Leyland PD2/27 models with Metro-Cammell bodies delivered in 1961 introduced a feature new to Bolton in that they were provided with full fronts, partly utilising the earlier Leyland design of enclosed bonnet, often referred to as the 'tin front'. Number 142 is shown opposite the Central Library, about to depart for Plodder Lane on service 5. They were delivered in the cherry and cream livery, introduced by Mr Bennett. Unlike the previous scheme, this livery did nothing to alleviate the ungainly appearance of this style of body. *(RM)*

By contrast the East Lancashire-bodied Leyland PD3/4 models delivered that same year retained the traditional Leyland radiator and this, together with the stylish body design, made them classic vehicles. Number 157 was one of eleven numbered 151-161. They also carried the cherry and cream livery when new. *(RM)*

Also in 1961 there was something of a surprise when six AEC Regent V double-deckers were received with Metro-Cammell bodies. These were the first AEC double-deckers to be operated by Bolton, apart from the experimental 'Q' type in the 'thirties. They were numbered 162-167, and No. 164 is shown parked at the Westhoughton terminus of service 39 awaiting time for the return journey to Bolton in April 1962. The photograph below shows a nearside view of the same vehicle parked in Bolton in June 1965. They also were delivered in the cherry and cream livery as seen. Paper adverts and bus washers did not always make a happy combination. *(RM)*

Overleaf: 1962 was notable as the year when the last front engined buses entered the Bolton fleet and also for another change of livery. All were Leyland PD3A/2 models with the body contract split between East Lancashire and Metro-Cammell. Number 170 with ELCB body is shown photographed when new. Numbers 179, 181, 183 and 184 all entered service in 1963. *(STA)*

The cherry and cream livery was applied to older buses as they became due for repaint. Leyland PD2/4 No 391 above, displays this as does 1949 Leyland PD2/4 No 403 below. The appearance was very similar in style, albeit with different colours, to the liveries at Great Yarmouth and Plymouth where Mr Bennet had been, prior to his appointment at Bolton. *(RM)*

A comparison of body styles is provided by these two views – at the top East Lancashire-bodied number 169 is shown leaving Moor Lane Bus Station for Withens Estate in April 1962 shortly after entering service. In the lower view, clearly at the same place Metro-Cammell bodied No 184 is seen. This was numerically the last front engined double-decker to enter the fleet and was photographed in March 1963. In each case the upper-deck front is instantly recognisable as being its manufacturers standard design. *(RM)*

The new livery reverted to the traditional colours of maroon and cream, but with greater proportions of cream. It was also applied to older buses, as had been the cherry and cream scheme. This 1956 Bond-bodied Leyland PD2/13 was still in the latter colours when in use as a training vehicle. It is shown here in Shiffnall Street Depot. Comparison can be made with sister vehicle No. 68, carrying the more attractive later livery, and photographed in service passing the Odeon cinema en route to Wingates. The **Carry On** team are in full swing. *(BD)*

Two Leyland PD2s, both with Metro-Cammell bodies, but showing contrasting styles. In the upper photograph No. 125, dating from 1957, has traditional radiator and rear entrance open platform bodywork, which was the 'norm' for British double-deckers for many years. The lower photograph shows No. 138 dating from 1961, only two years later but with full front, concealed radiator and front entrance body. In the distance one of Ribble's large fleet of Leyland double-deckers moves away from the camera. *(BD both)*

A similar situation to the previous page shows comparison between East Lancashire Coachbuilders bodies. In the upper photograph No. 130, with traditional radiator but with one of the first forward-entrance double-deck bodies supplied to Bolton, contrasts with No. 168 below, supplied in 1963 and also with front entrance but with the final style of concealed radiator used by Leyland Motors Ltd. Bolton's double-deckers had been fitted with rear entrances from the beginning, with the Leviathans and then the various Titan models, with only the solitary AEC 'Q' type of the 'thirties breaking the mould. *(BD both)*

The Arrival of the Atlantean

By 1963 the rear engined double-decker was establishing itself and was popular with traffic departments because of its increased seating capacity, but often not popular with engineers because of its increased complexity and, in some cases, reliability problems.

There were of course bodies on the market to suit these chassis, the vast majority of which could be best described as uninspiring, and offerings such as these were clearly not acceptable to Mr Bennett.

It so happened that Liverpool City Transport, a large operator with strong buying power, was also not impressed with these designs and negotiated with Metro-Cammell for a revised design. The outcome was a sleek modern attractive design with good standard of interior finish and it was made available to other operators. Only two operators availed themselves of this 'Liverpool' design, one being Bolton which received seven examples in 1963 on Leyland Atlantean PDR1/1 chassis and the other being neighbouring Bury Corporation Transport which received 15 in 1963.

Whilst the design was good, it seems that Mr Bennett still had his own ideas on bus body design and wanted to develop these. To this end, he turned to East Lancashire Coachbuilders, already established with Bolton and indeed other operators as a quality bus builder and with a reputation for their readiness to build what the customer wanted. From these negotiations, a new body design emerged which was modern, functional and attractive and which was to become the standard for Bolton for the remainder of its existence as an operator.

A total of 102 examples of this design were purchased between 1963 and 1969, some of the last batch being delivered direct to SELNEC. Neepsend Coachworks, Sheffield, an associated company of East Lancashire Coachbuilders built the bodies on four of the 1963 deliveries. In 1965, in addition to the bodies supplied by East Lancashire, there were eight examples with the 'Liverpool' style of Metro-Cammell body. Over the years there were minor differences in the body style, examples of which are illustrated in the photographic coverage.

With the introduction of the rear engine double-decker came a new destination indicator layout comprising at the front, two single line blinds one above the other to the left of a large three track, service number display and with a three track service number display at the side. The two single line destination displays were used in an unusual manner whereby each displayed opposite termini of the route.

There was a further link with Southern Ireland in 1964 when Leyland Atlantean No. 200 was hired to Coras Iompair Eireann and used on Dublin City Services.

In 1965 Mr Bennett left Bolton to succeed Mr Albert Neal as General Manager of Manchester City Transport and took with him his flair for design which later materialised as the 'Mancunian' double-decker. He was succeeded at Bolton by his deputy Mr Jim Batty who had been at Bolton since 1930 and remained as General Manager until the undertaking was absorbed into SELNEC as from 1st November 1969.

Jim Batty, who was appointed General Manager after Mr Bennett went to Manchester. Mr Batty became Divisional Manager when SELNEC Northern were based in the former Bolton offices in 1970. He then became Director/General Manager of SELNEC Northern in the reorganisation into three companies which took place in March 1971. In March 2007 Jim was one of the special guests at a reunion of enthusiasts and others to recall the events of 60 years previously when Bolton and Salford's last trams had run. *(STA)*

The real successor to the Q type double-decker was the Atlantean. Once again the doorway was right at the front, directly alongside the driver and fully under his supervision. Unlike the Q, Atlanteans were fitted with platform doors for increased passenger comfort and safety. The more important difference, however, was that the engine – or power-pack as it now became known – was hung at the back of the chassis, completely outside the passenger area, thus leaving the interior free of intrusions other than the wheelarches, and thus greatly increasing the seating capacity. The fitment of shrouds above the engine compartment was another step in improving the body design. Around 62 seats had been possible in front-engined vehicles such as the PD2s, and 74 in the PD3s, it was now possible to fit seventy-eight seats within the bodyshell. Union resistance to this greater carrying capacity in some fleets was considerable; in Manchester their new fleet of Atlanteans stood idle and unused for many months before agreement was reached because there had not previously been any 30ft-long vehicles in the fleet. When one-man operation of double-deckers became legal, a pay package for driver-only operation spelled the end of the conductors.

Engineers also faced challenges with the new model which, at first, was very unreliable. Bolton, like several other large operators, decided to wait and see; it continued taking front-engined buses into the fleet almost four years after the Atlantean's introduction, thereby avoiding many of the worst of the initial problems. Finally, almost in desperation, the engineers from the newly-formed PTEs, led by Oldham's Harry Taylor, produced a specification for a modified Atlantean which Leyland adopted and introduced as the AN68, giving a clue as to how long it took to resolve matters. Thereafter the Atlantean became a very reliable machine and only the introduction of EU emission and other directives forced cessation of its manufacture for the UK market. *(STA)*

A major change in the fleet took place in 1963 when the first rear-engined vehicles entered service. They were Leyland Atlanteans of type PDR1/1 and eight carried bodies built by East Lancashire Coachbuilders to a design which had been developed in conjunction with Mr Bennett, the Bolton General Manager. They were numbered 185-192 and No. 190 is shown in Deansgate, Bolton. (*STA*)

In addition to the Atlanteans with East Lancashire Coachbuilders bodies, Bolton took seven examples with bodies by Metropolitan-Cammell. These were to a design which the builder had introduced in conjunction with and to the requirements of Liverpool City Transport. Notice the lack of engine shrouds in this view although it was much more stylish than the builder's standard design; the Bolton examples were numbered 193-199. Number 194 is shown in Trinity Street, about to pass Holy Trinity Church. (*RM*)

An interesting comparison is provided in this photograph taken by East Lancashire Coachbuilders showing one of the last Atlanteans supplied to Bolton alongside one of the 'Mancunian' double-deckers, also with East Lancashire Coachbuilders body, and which Mr Bennett had introduced at Manchester. In both cases the bright livery is eye-catching and inviting – the shaped windscreen on the Bolton vehicle was adopted to reduce build up of road dirt on the bodies by altering the air-flow around the front of the vehicle. Other bodybuilders were taking similar steps and the whole industry was generally trying to attract more passengers to its vehicles. *(STA)*

Connections with Coras Iompair Eireann were resumed when Bolton Atlantean No. 200 was loaned to CIE for trial on Dublin City Services. It is shown being loaded onto the ferry for the journey to Ireland. *(STA)*

The body contract for the twelve Atlanteans supplied in 1964 was placed with East Lancashire Coachbuilders. They were numbered 200-211, but the bodies on four of them, numbered 204-206 and 211 were built by Neepsend Coachworks of Sheffield. Neepsend was an associate company of East Lancashire Coachbuilders which, at this particular time, was part of the Cravens Group, who had of course bodied the large batch of Crossley chassis supplied to Bolton in 1946/7. *(HPC)*

From time to time ELCB sub-contracted work to Neepsend who, as mentioned above, occupied premises in Sheffield. These bodies would be built in the Penistone Road works and were built to the East Lancashire Coachbuilders design and drawings. Number 204 is shown above, and No. 211 below. *(HPC)*

The first single-decker to be received since 1956 arrived in 1962 and was an East Lancashire Coachbuilders-bodied Leyland Leopard L2 with fleet number 12. It had dual-purpose high-back seating for 41 passengers together with curved glass cantrails. It is shown above on more mundane duties leaving Moor Lane Bus Station for Affetside, and followed by a Leyland PD2/4 still in the maroon-and-three-cream-bands livery which now looks very dated by comparison with the Leopard. In the lower view at the other terminus the era of renovation and upgrading of the old cottages has clearly begun. *(BD, STA courtesy BCVM)*.

Number 12 was followed in 1964 by numbers 14 and 15 – there was no number 13! These were Leyland PSU3/4R models with East Lancashire bodies seating 49 and provided with both front and centre doors. Number 15, photographed when new, shows off the dual doorways whilst No. 14 is shown at Moor Lane Bus Station awaiting departure to Borough Hospital in April 1966. *(STA)*

Numbers 16 and 17, also supplied in 1964, were on shorter Leyland Leopard L2 chassis with ELCB bodies seating only 43. Number 16 is shown in Moor Lane en route to Affetside in May 1969. *(RM)*

A pristine new vehicle and lots of men with notebooks and cameras can only mean one thing – an enthusiasts' outing to Bolton's Shifnall Street depot for an official visit. Number 218, with body by East Lancashire Coachbuilders, waits patiently outside the depot on 8th August 1965. *(KWS)*

Three ladies chat, no doubt unaware that they have been caught on camera as our photographer captures No. 220, one of the 1965 Atlanteans with Metropolitan-Cammell bodies, heading for Johnson Fold on service 19. *(BD)*

A number of the East Lancashire Coachbuilders-bodied Atlanteans delivered in 1967, including No. 267, seen (top) when it was new and before entering service, did not have sliding ventilators to the upper-saloon windows. By contrast, No, 271, (centre) numerically the last of the 1967, delivery was one of those which retained them. It is seen in operation passing the Odeon Cinema on service 46. *(STA upper, BD centre)*

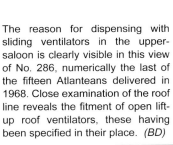

The reason for dispensing with sliding ventilators in the upper-saloon is clearly visible in this view of No. 286, numerically the last of the fifteen Atlanteans delivered in 1968. Close examination of the roof line reveals the fitment of open lift-up roof ventilators, these having been specified in their place. *(BD)*

In August 1969, just two months before the takeover by SELNEC, 1956 Bond-bodied Leyland PD2/13 leaves Moor Lane Bus Station for Radcliffe on service 36, and passes 1957 Daimler CVG6 No 95 with Metro-Cammell body. It was a sad day for most enthusiasts when the traditional radiators disappeared, leaving buses faceless and uninteresting in many people's opinion. *(RM)*

This Bolton Atlantean shows Manchester as its destination on service No. 8 but it would not reach Manchester. It is shown at its southern terminus, Victoria Bus Station, Salford, with the river Irwell forming the boundary between the two cities hidden behind the bus shelter. It was common practice in those days to show **Manchester** as the destination on vehicles arriving from outside the Salford boundary and terminating here or at the adjacent Greengate, often described as the most dismal bus station in the country. The Salford Atlantean in the background is an example of the type of body 'styling' Ralph Bennett was determined to do without! *(STA)*

The end of an era. The last vehicles ordered by Bolton prior to the takeover by SELNEC were fifteen Leyland Atlantean PDR1A/1 models with bodies by East Lancashire Coachbuilders. Although to the same basic outline as earlier models there were notable differences. The lack of sliding ventilators to the windows is noticeable as are the sloping window pillars. They were also dual-door models. A number, including No. 296 shown here at Moor Lane Bus Station, were delivered direct to SELNEC, having arrived after the takeover date, and thus do not carry the Bolton crest and lettering. (BD)

The End of an Era

The date 1st November 1969 brought to an end a period of 70 years during which Bolton Transport had served the people of Bolton and the surrounding area very well. The politicians then interfered and the South East Lancashire and North East Cheshire (SELNEC) Passenger Transport Executive was created. Since that time, with further political interference, privatisation has come along and again brought with it a change of operator. No doubt the people of Bolton will have their opinions, sentiment apart, as to whether or not these changes brought improvements to the services provided for so many years by their own Bolton Transport Department.

The offices in Bradshawgate now became the Headquarters of the new SELNEC Northern Division, taking in the former municipal fleets of Bolton, Bury, Leigh, Ramsbottom and Rochdale, with three Bolton depots and workshops also remaining in use for the new organisation. Former Bolton staff in key positions included Jim Batty (see page 131) and Tony Harrison, former Chief Executive of Bolton Council, who rather surprisingly, became SELNEC's Director General.

Even with the changeover to SELNEC it was some time before the evidence of Bolton Transport disappeared. Initially the fleet numbers on vehicles were painted out and small stick-on temporary labels carrying the Bolton fleet number, applied at the front pending the application of SELNEC numbers. Even this took place over a considerable period and some vehicles continued to display their Bolton numbers into 1971. The SELNEC numbers were derived by adding 6000 to Bolton single-deck numbers and 6500 to double-deck numbers. In 1973 there were still vehicles carrying the Bolton livery, albeit with SELNEC legal lettering.

After the formation of SELNEC and the adoption of the new livery, Bolton's vehicles due for repaint, and with reasonable life-expectancy in the fleet, were painted in the new colours. The first ones appeared in the summer of 1970. After SELNEC administration became divisional, SELNEC NORTHERN vehicles carried a magenta *S* as shown in this (later) 1973 view of UBN 915, built in 1962 as number 182, but now numbered 6682. *(JAS left; MB below)*

APPENDIX 1   TRAM FLEET LIST

YEAR	FLEET Nos.	DETAILS	TRUCKS	TYPE	BODY	NOTES
1900	1 - 40	Double-Deck Open Top	4 Wheel	Brill 21 E	ERTCW	
	41 - 48	Double-Deck Open Top	4 Wheel	Brill 21 E	ERTCW	
	49	Double-Deck OpenTop	Bogie	Brill 22 E	ERTCW	
1901	50 - 59	Double-Deck Open Top	Bogie	Brill 22 E	ERTCW	
	60 - 81	Double-Deck Canopy	Bogie	Brill 22 E	ERTCW	
1903	82 - 86	Double-Deck Open Top	4 Wheel	Brill 21 E	ERTCW	
1906	87 - 96	Double-Deck Open Top	4 Wheel	Brill 21 E	Brush	
1910-12	97 - 103	Double-Deck Covered Top	Bogie	Brill 22 E	UEC	
	104 - 106	Single-Deck Combination	Bogie	Brill 22 E	UEC	
	107 - 112	Double-Deck Covered Top	Bogie	Brill 22 E	UEC	
1921	113 - 120	Double-Deck Covered Top	Bogie	Brill 22 E	Eng.Electric	
1923	121 - 130	Double-Deck Covered Top	Bogie	Brill 22E	Eng.Electric	(1)
1924	131 - 138	Double-Deck Covered Top	4 Wheel	Brill 21E	Brush	(2)
1927	139 - 150	Double-Deck Fully Enclosed	Bogie	Brill 22 E	Eng. Electric	(3)
1928	104 - 106	Double-Deck Fully Enclosed	Bogie	Brill 22E	Eng. Electric	(3; 4)
1933	33 - 40	Double-Deck Covered Top	Bogie	Burnley	Milnes	(5)

Ex Bury Corporation

YEAR	FLEET Nos.	DETAILS	TRUCKS	TYPE	BODY	NOTES
1943	331	Double-Deck Fully Enclosed	4 Wheel	Maguire	Bury Corp'n.	
	451 - 453	Double-Deck Enclosed	Bogie	Eng. Electric	Eng. Electric	

Notes
(1) Trucks supplied by Bolton Corporation.
(2) Ex Sunderland District
(3) Brill bogies built by Brush
(4) Bodies supplied by English Electric; possibly used parts from original bogies of cars 104 -106
(5) Ex-South Lancashire Transport.

In 1940 the tram fleet was renumbered by the addition of 300 to existing numbers.
With the exception of the cars built by Brush and Milnes, all Bolton's trams were built in
Strand Road, Preston – the name of the company changed over the years as shown in the table.

Car 30 in its final form illustrating how the open-topper had evolved, through a balcony-top, to the enclosed upper-deck seen here following the purchase of the all-enclosed bogie cars in 1927. *(66 Group)*

APPENDIX 2   BUS FLEET LIST

YEAR	REG. Nos.	FLEET Nos.	CHASSIS	BODY	BODY TYPE	NOTES.
1904	BN 140		Stirling	?		
1907	BN 229		Darracq-Serpollet	?		Steam
1908	LN 9397		Straker Squire	?		Hired
1908	LN 9398		Commer Cars	?		Hired
1924	BN 7102-4	1-3	Leyland C7	Leyland	B--R	
1924	BN 7267-8	4-5	Leyland C7	Leyland	B--R	
1924	BN 7725-8	6-9	Leyland SG9	Leyland	B--R	
1926	BN 9364	10	Leyland LG1	Leyland	H52ROS	
1926	BN 9354	11	Leyland LG1	Leyland	H52ROS	
1926	BN 9380-2	12-14	Leyland LG1	Leyland	H52ROS	
1926	BN 9355	15	Leyland PLSC1	Leyland	B29R	
1926	BN 9383-91	16-24	Leyland PLSC1	Leyland	B29R	
1927	WH 201-5	25-29	Leyland PLSC3	Leyland	B34R	
1927	WH 206-10	30-34	Leyland PLSP1	Leyland	H29/26R	
1928	WH 631-2	35-36	Leyland PLSC3	Leyland	B32D	
1928	WH 801-10	37-46	Leyland TD1	Leyland	L27/24RO	
1928	WH 1181-5	47-51	Leyland TS2	Leyland	B29R	
1929	WH 1353	2	AEC 426	?	B32	(1)
1929	WH 1299	4	Leyland TS1	Harrington	C26D	(1)
1929	WH 1551-5	52-56	Leyland TD1	Leyland	L27/24ROS	
1930	TE 8290	3	Leyland TS1	Massey	B35F	(2)
1930	WH 2601-5	57-61	Leyland TD1	Roberts	L27/24ROS	
1931	WH 3301-2	5-6	Leyland TD1	Roberts	L24/24R	
1931	WH 3303-10	7-14	Leyland TD1	Leyland	L24/24R	
1933	WH 4850	2	AEC Q	MCCW	H32/28F	(3)
1933	WH 4211-20	62-71	Leyland TD2	B.& Edwards	L24/24R	
1933	WH 4901-5	72-76	Leyland TD3	B.& Edwards	H28/24R	
1933	WH 4906-7	77-78	Leyland TD3	Weymann	H28/24R	
1933	WH 4908-10	79-81	Leyland TD3	E.Electric	H28/24R	
1934	WH 5401-5	82-86	Leyland TD3c	B.&Edwards	H28/24R	
1934	WH 5501-5	87-91	Leyland TD3c	B.&Edwards	H27/24R	
1934	WH 5801-5	92-96	Leyland TS6c	Burlingham	B30R	
1935	WH 6851-3	97-99	Leyland TS7c	Massey	B30R	
1935	WH 6854-6	100-102	Leyland TS7c	Leyland	B30R	
1936	WH 6857-66	15-24	Leyland TD4c	Roberts	L26/26R	
1936	WH 7801-5	25-29	Leyland TD4c	Leyland	L26/26R	
1936	WH 7806-20	30-44	Leyland TD4c	Massey	L26/26R	
1937	WH 9201-15	103-117	Leyland TD5c	Leyland	H28/26R	
1937	WH 9216-25	118-127	Leyland TD5c	Massey	H28/26R	
1937	WH 9501-5	128-132	Leyland TD5c	Massey	H28/26R	
1937	WH 9506-15	133-142	Leyland TD5c	Leyland	H28/26R	
1938	ABN 401-402	1-2	Leyland TS8c	Park Royal	DP32R	
1938	ABN 403-404	3-4	Leyland TS8c	Massey	B32R	
1938	ABN 405-414	143-152	Leyland TD5c	East Lancs	H28/26R	
1939	ABN 601-640	153-192	Leyland TD5c	Massey	H28/26R	
1940-2	AWH 931-955	193-217	Leyland TD5c	Massey	H28/26R	
1940-2	BBN 176-200	218-242	Leyland TD5c	Massey	H28/26R	
1946	BWH 60-126	246-312	Crossley DD42/3	Cravens	H30/26R	
1946	BWH 127-134	313-320	Crossley DD42/3	Crossley	H30/26R	

APPENDIX 2   BUS FLEET LIST

YEAR	REG. Nos.	FLEET Nos.	CHASSIS	BODY	BODY TYPE	NOTES.
1947	BWH 822-836	321-335	Leyland PD1/2	NCME	H30/26R	
1947	CBN 101-115	336-350	Leyland PD1/2	Crossley	H30/26R	
1948	CWH 701-750	351-400	Leyland PD2/4	Leyland	H30/26R	
1949	DBN 975-978	5-8	Crossley SD42/7	Crossley	B32R	
1949	DBN 304-353	401-450	Leyland PD2/4	Leyland	H30/26R	
1955	GWH 516	9	Leyland PSU1/14	East Lancs	B43F	
1955	GWH 501-515	51-65	Leyland PD2/13	MCCW	H31/27R	
1955	JBN 140	66	Leyland PD2/12	Bond	H32/28R	
1956	JBN 141	10	Leyland PSU1/13	Bond	B44F	
1956	JBN 142	11	Bedford SBO	Duple	C41F	
1956	JBN 143-151	67-75	Leyland PD2/13	Bond	H33/27R	
1956	JBN 152-160	76-84	Leyland PD2/13	MCCW	H33/27R	
1957	KWH 565-574	85-94	Daimler CVG6K	East Lancs	H35/28RD	
1957	KWH 575-585	95-105	Daimler CVG6K	MCCW	H34/28R	
1958	MBN 161-167	106-112	Daimler CVG6-30	MCCW	H41/33R	
1958	MBN 168-177	113-122	Leyland PD3/5	East Lancs	H41/33R	
1959	NBN 431-435	123-127	Leyland PD2/37	MCCW	H34/28R	
1959	NBN 436-440	128-132	Leyland PD3/4	East Lancs	H41/32F	
1960	PBN 661-668	143-150	Daimler CVG6-30	East Lancs	H41/32F	
1961	PBN 651-660	133-142	Leyland PD2/27	MCCW	FH35/27F	
1961	SBN 751-761	151-161	Leyland PD3/4	East Lancs	H41/32F	
1961	SBN 762-767	162-167	AEC Regent V	MCCW	H40/32F	
1962	UWH 322	12	Leyland L2	East Lancs	DP41F	
1962	UBN 901-909	168-176	Leyland PD3A/2	East Lancs	FH41/32F	
1962	UBN 910-917	177-184	Leyland PD3A/2	MCCW	FH41/31F	
1963	UWH 185-192	185-192	Leyland PDR1/1	East Lancs	H45/33F	
1963	UWH 193-199	193-199	Leyland PDR1/1	MCCW	H43/35F	
1964	YBN 14-15	14-15	Leyland PSU3/4R	East Lancs	B49D	
1964	YBN 16-17	16-17	Leyland L2	East Lancs	B43D	
1964	ABN 200-211B	200-211	Leyland PDR1/1	East Lancs	H45/33F	(4)
1965	ABN 212-218C	212-218	Leyland PDR1/1	East Lancs	H45/33F	
1965	ABN 219-226C	219-226	Leyland PDR1/1	MCCW	H45/32F	
1965	FBN 227-234C	227-234	Leyland PDR1/1	East Lancs	H45/33F	
1965	FBN 235D	235	Leyland PDR1/1	East Lancs	H45/33F	
1965	FBN 236C	236	Leyland PDR1/1	East Lancs	H45/33F	
1965	FBN 237D	237	Leyland PDR1/1	East Lancs	H45/33F	
1965	FBN 238C	238	Leyland PDR1/1	East Lancs	H45/33F	
1965	FBN 239D	239	Leyland PDR1/1	East Lancs	H45/33F	
1965	FBN 240-241C	240-241	Leyland PDR1/1	East Lancs	H45/33F	
1966	GBN 242-256D	242-256	Leyland PDR1/1	East Lancs	H45/33F	
1967	HWH 257-271F	257-271	Leyland PDR1/1	East Lancs	H45/33F	
1968	MWH 272-286G	272-286	Leyland PDR1A/1	East Lancs	H45/33F	
1969	OBN 287-301H	287-301	Leyland PDR1A/1	East Lancs	H43/29D	(5)

Notes :-
(1) Ex JR Tognarelli, Bolton 12/29 Number 4 converted to B32F before entering service.
(2) Ex Freeman (Silver Star) Chorley. Rebuilt to B32F before entering service 14/1/31
(3) AEC Q No. 2 retained this fleet number until sold despite there being another No. 2 in 1938
(4) Nos. 204-206/11 were built at East Lancs. associated company, Neepsend Coachworks, Sheffield.
(5) Nos. 287/291/295/300 were new to Bolton. Remainder were delivered to SELNEC.
    There were also four Roe-bodied Leyland TTB4 trolleybuses, numbered 48-51, garaged and maintained by
    the SLT Company on behalf of Bolton Corporation who owned them, and used exclusively on the former
    Leigh-Bolton tram route until SLT abandoned its trolleybus system on 31st August 1958.

APPENDIX 3

SCHEDULE OF WARTIME LOANS FROM BOLTON

OPERATOR	F/Nos.	DATES	F/Nos.	DATES	F/Nos.	DATES	NOTES
LUT	63	10/40-11/42	64-9	10/40-01/43	71	10/40-04/47	
	75	02/43-?	80	02/43-01/46	25	04/41-11/44	
	27	04/41-01/46	28	05/410-2/46	30/35	04/41-11/44	
	32	04/41-04/45	33	04/41-08/45	38	04/41-11/44	
Crosville	70	10/42-	16	12/40-1943	20	12/40-1943	(1)
	65/9	02/43-	18/19	12/40-1943	23	12/40-1943	(2)
Cumberland	21	05/43-2/46	90	05/43-2/46	124	05/43-12/44	
BMMO	76	11/41-01/42	79	08/41-02/42	84	11/41-01/42	
	87	07/41-01/42					
Harper Bros	83	06/41-08/45					
LPTB	72-91	01/41-08/41	15/21	01/41-08/41	22/24	01/41-08/41	
Liverpool	86	03/42-11/42	90	03/42-05/42	118	02/42-11/42	
	124	02/42-03/43					
Widnes	72	10/42-?	79	12/44-05/45	86	11/42-11/44	
	26	05/41-11/45	29	05/41-11/44			
St. Helens	31	12/41-12/45	37	12/41-11/44			
Grimsby	40	08/43-11/44	118	08/43-11/43			
Coventry	15/17	12/41-08/45	21	12/41-06/42	22	12/41-11/44	
	24	01/43-11/44	34	12/41-08/45	36/39	12/41-11/44	
	41	02/42-08/45	42	02/42-11/44	43	12/41-08/45	
	44	12/41-08/43	72	04/42-06/42	73/74	02/42-11/44	
	75	12/41-02/43	76	01/42-10/46	77	02/42-01/46	
	78	08/41-11/44	79	02/42-12/44	80	12/41-02/43	
	81	10/41-01/46	82	12/41-11/44	84	01/42-01/46	
	85	10/41-03/46	87	01/42-11/44	88	01/42-03/46	
	89	12/41-10/46	91	01/42-11/44			

Notes
(1) No. 70 was purchased by Crosville in 02/45.
(2) Nos. 65 and 69 were purchased by Crosville in 1944

APPENDIX 4   WARTIME & SUBSEQUENT REBODYINGS

TABLE 1 NORTHERN COACHBUILDERS ORDER DATED 17.10.44. INCREASED 6.1.45 TO 6

New	Reg. No.	Fleet No.	Chassis	Body	Relicensed	Body To	Date	Notes
1936	WH 6857	15	TD4c	UH30/26R	5/45	166 (ABN 614)	3/50	
1936	WH 6859	17	TD4c	UH30/26R	7/45	214 (AWH 952)	8/48	
1936	WH 6860	18	TD4c	UH30/26R	7/45	121 (WH 9219)	9/48	
1936	WH 7808	32	TD4c	UH30/26R	7/45	190 (ABN 638)	3/50	
1936	WH 7809	33	TD4c	UH30/26R	7/45	191 (ABN 639)	3/50	
1936	WH 5402	83	TD4c	UH30/26R	7/45	129 (WH 9502)	8/48	

TABLE 2 NORTHERN COACHBUILDERS ORDER DATED 14.3.45

New	Reg. No.	Fleet No.	Chassis	Body	Relicensed	Body to	Date	Notes
1936	WH 6861	19	TD4c	UH30/26R	7/45	207 (AWH 945)	-/49	
1933	WH 4905	76	TD3	H30/26R	8/46	212 (AWH 950)	-/49	(3)
1933	WH 4909	80	TD3	UH30/26R	1/46	124 (WH 9222)	-/49	(1)
1933	WH 4910	81	TD3	UH30/26R	2/46	131 (WH 9504)	6/49	(1)
1934	WH 5403	84	TD3c	UH30/26R	1/46	200 (AWH 938)	-/49	(1)
1934	WH 5404	85	TD3c	UH30/26R	3/46	148 (ABN 410)	-/49	(1)
1934	WH 5501	87	TD3c	UH30/26R	12/45	149 (ABN 411)	-/49	(1)
1934	WH 5502	88	TD3c	UH30/26R	3/46	147 (ABN 409)	-/49	(1)
1934	WH 5503	89	TD3c	H30/26R	8/46	211 (AWH 949)	-/49	(3)
1935	WH 6851	97	TS7c	H30/26R	10/46	131 (WH 9504)	4/53	(2)
1935	WH 6852	98	TS7c	H30/26R	8/46	195 (AWH 933)	4/53	(2)
1935	WH 6853	99	TS7c	H30/26R	7/46	204 (AWH 942)	4/53	(2)

This order also covered the rebuilding of Nos. 23,41,75,79,86. Number 87 was originally to have been a rebuild.

TABLE 3 NORTHERN COACHBUILDERS ORDER DATED 24.10.45

New	Reg. No.	Fleet No.	Chassis	Body	Relicensed	Body to	Date	Notes
1936	WH 6866	24	TD4c	H30/26R	8/46	203 (AWH 941)	3/50	(3)
1936	WH 7813	37	TD4c	H30/26R	7/46	194 (AWH 932)	3/50	(3)
1933	WH 4901	72	TD3	H30/26R	9/46	210 (AWH 948)	-/49	(3)
1934	WH 5505	91	TD3c	H30/26R	10/46	205 (AWH 943	-/49	(3)

TABLE 4 EAST LANCASHIRE COACHBUILDERS ORDER DATED 17.10.44

New	Reg. No.	Fleet No.	Chassis	Body	Relicensed	Body To	Date	Notes
1936	WH 7807	31	TD4c	H30/26R	8/46	201 (AWH 939)	3/50	(4)
1936	WH 7810	34	TD4c	H30/26R	3/46	202 (AWH 940)	3/50	(4)
1936	WH 7811	35	TD4c	H30/26R	3/46	215 (AWH 953)	3/46	(4)
1936	WH 7814	38	TD4c	H30/26R	3/46	196 (AWH 934)	3/50	(4)
1936	WH 7819	43	TD4c	H30/26R	3/46	206 (AWH 944)	3/50	(4)
1936	WH 7820	44	TD4c	H30/26R	3/46	198 (AWH 936)	3/50	(4)

TABLE 5 OTHER BODY CHANGES

Reg. No.	Fleet No.	Chassis	Body	Ex Bus	Relicensed	Notes
AWH 946	208	TD5	Leyland	140	-/53	
AWH 654	216	TD5	NCB	194	9/53	
BBN 184	226	TD7c	Leyland	26	12/48	

Notes.
(1) Indicates relaxed Utility Body
(2) Renumbered 243-5 on rebodying as double deckers
(3). Indicates Postwar Body Style. A five months delay was incurred when NCB, without reference to Bolton, decided to introduce their postwar body design.
(4) East Lancashire Coachbuilders did not build to the Wartime Utility Specification.
Following the decision, in November 1945, to change the light red bands to cream, five gallons of cream paint were sent to NCB with the request that they return their stock of light red.

Appendix 5   Bus Routes as at 21st May 1958

1	Green Lane - Chorley Old Road (Moss Bank Way)
2	Townleys - Barrow Bridge via Chorley Old Road.
3	Townleys - Rushey Fold Lane via Vernon Street.
4	Townleys - Barrow bridge via Mount Street.
5	Markland Hill - Farnworth (Highfield Rd./Tigg Fold Rd.), joint with LUT.
6	Moor Lane - Harwood (Nab Gate) via Thicketford Road.
6	Moor Lane - Padbury Way via Thicketford Road.
7	Moor Lane - Harwood (Nab Gate) via Tonge Moor Road.
8	Thynne Street - Manchester (Victoria Bus Station), joint with LUT and Salford.
9	Moor Lane - Ainsworth
10	Moor Lane - Crompton Way (Blackburn Road)
11	Markland Hill - Crompton Way (Circular)
12	Thynne Street - Salford (Greengate) via Little Hulton, joint with LUT and Salford
14	Moor Lane - Darcy Lever.
15	Moor Lane - Wigan via Lostock Junction, joint with LUT and Wigan
16	Horwich - Leigh via Wingates, Westhoughton, Atherton, joint with LUT and Leigh.
17	Howell Croft South - Daubhill Station.
17A	Howell Croft South - Hulton Lane.
17B	Howell Croft South - Four Lane Ends.
17C	Howell Croft South - Leigh via Atherton, joint with SLT.
18	Trinity Street - Ivy Road.
19	Trinity Street - Doffcocker.
20	Trinity Street - Johnson Fold Estate.
21	Great Moor Street - Crompton Avenue.
22	Great Moor Street - Blenheim Road.
23	Great Moor Street - Breightmet (Coach & Horses).
23T	Great Moor Street - Bury via Breightmet, joint with Bury.
24	Trinity Street - Halliwell (Moss Bank Way)
24	Trinity Street - Eskrick Street.
25	Trinity Street - Smithills Hall.
25	Trinity Street - Colliers Row School.
28	Trinity Street - Seymour Road.
29	Trinity Street - Andrew Lane.
30	Trinity Street - Dunscar.
31	Trinity Street - Eagley Mills.
32	Trinity Street - De Haviland Works, Lostock.
32	Horwich (Old Lord's Estate) - De Haviland Works via Chorley Old Road.
33	Trinity Street - Horwich (Entrance to Lever Park Avenue).
34	Trinity Street - Albert Road.
35	Trinity Street - Horwich (Old Lord's Estate).

Appendix 5   Bus Routes as at 21st May 1958

36	Moor Lane - Radcliffe Bus Station.
37	Little Lever (Coronation Square) - Breightmet (Coach & Horses).
38	Howell Croft South - Deane (Hulton Lane).
39	Howell Croft South - Westhoughton (Birch Avenue) joint with LUT.
40	Moor Lane - Withins Estate.
41	Thynne Street - Eccles Bus Station, joint with LUT.
42	Great Moor Street - Walkden, joint with LUT
43	Great Moor Street - Farnworth (Black Horse), joint with SLT.
44	Great Moor Street - Moses Gate.
48	Moor Lane - Borough Hospital (Hulton Lane).
49	Thynne Street - Union Road Mills.
50	Moor Lane - Warrington, joint with LUT.
51	Thynne Street - Little Lever - Stopes.
52	Thynne Street - Bury (Broad Street) via Little lever, joint with Bury.
53	Moor Lane - Affetside.
54	Moor Lane - Oldhams Estate (Selkirk Road).
55	Moor Lane - Belmont.
57	Howell Croft South - Lever Edge Lane (Hurlston Road) via Morris Green.
61	Tonge Moor or Hall I' th' Wood or Crompton Way to Higher Swan Lane/Lever Edge Lane.
62	Tonge Moor or Hall I 'th' Wood or Crompton Way - Rishton Lane / Lever Edge Lane.
63	Higher Swan Lane/Lever Edge Lane - Tonge Moor via Rishton Lane.
63	Rishton Lane/ Lever Edge Lane - Tonge Moor via Higher Swan Lane.
64	Higher Swan Lane/Lever Edge Lane - Hall I' th' Wood via Rishton Lane.
64	Rishton Lane/Lever Edge Lane - Hall I' th' Wood via Higher Swan Lane.
65	Higher Swan Lane/Lever Edge Lane - Crompton Way via Rishton Lane.
65	Rishton Lane/Lever Edge Lane - Crompton Way via Higher Swan Lane.
122	Moor Lane - Chorley - Southport, joint with Ribble.
122	Moor Lane - Horwich (Mechanics Institute) via Bottom o' th' Moor, joint with Ribble.
215	Moor Lane - Blackburn Railway Station via Astley Bridge, joint with Ribble.
225	Moor Lane - Blackburn Railway Station via Tonge Moor, joint with Ribble.
B15	Moor Lane - Dimple via Astley Bridge, joint with Ribble.
B25	Moor Lane - Dunscar War Memorial via Tonge Moor, joint with Ribble.
B35	Moor Lane - Dimple via Tonge Moor.
-	De Haviland Works, Lostock - Daubhill.
X66	Blackburn - Manchester, joint with Ribble and LUT.

Bolton's local buses

All buses shown running to Bolton Town Centre terminate in Moor Lane Bus Station 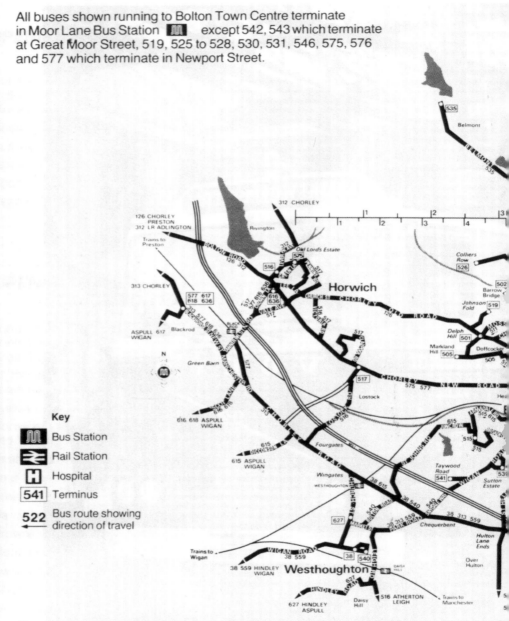 except 542, 543 which terminate at Great Moor Street, 519, 525 to 528, 530, 531, 546, 575, 576 and 577 which terminate in Newport Street.

Key

🚌	Bus Station
🚆	Rail Station
H	Hospital
541	Terminus
522 ←	Bus route showing direction of travel

Bus Guides are available for all Greater Manchester Transport's Services. They are fr__ of times and routes. Bus Guides for local services are available from the Information O__ Moor Lane Bus Station, or by writing to—
The Publicity Officer, Greater Manchester Transport, 2 Devonshire Street North, Ardw__

Greater
Manchester
Transport

Lost Property Office
Moor Lane Bus Station
☎ Bolton 32361

273 RAMSBOTTOM
      RAWTENSTALL
      BURNLEY
565 TOTTINGTON
      BURY

564 TOTTINGTON
      WALSHAW

400 BURY
      ROCHDALE
      OLDHAM
      STOCKPORT
523 BURY

536 537 RADCLIFFE
         WHITEFIELD

510 RADCLIFFE
524 RADCLIFFE
      BURY

RADCLIFFE
483 BURY
493 WHITEFIELD

Trains to Manchester
8 SALFORD
   MANCHESTER
20 ECCLES
    CADISHEAD

12 38 WALKDEN
       SALFORD
       MANCHESTER

551 WALKDEN
573 LEIGH
584 SWINTON
      ATHERTON
      LEIGH

31 483
493 558
551 584

500 STRETFORD
      WYTHENSHAWE
      MANCHESTER AIRPORT
542 SWINTON
544 ECCLES
547 548 TRAFFORD PARK
571 LEIGH

Farnworth

e full details
n,
ester M12 6JS.

Timetable and fare enquiries
☎ ▦ 061-226 8181
   🖶 061-832 8353

April 1984

Bolton Corporation Tickets

The first recorded method of fare collection dates back to the horse tram period and did not in fact involve the issue of tickets, as a fare collection box patented by Joseph Kaye, was in use. Passengers deposited their fare through a slot in the top of the box which fell onto a glass sided tray visible to the conductor. After checking through the window that the correct fare had been paid, the conductor then operated a catch on the back of the container which dropped the coins into the bottom of the locked container. These fare boxes were introduced on 5th December 1888, when the routes, with the exception of that to Daubhill, were divided into three one penny one stages. The Daubhill service, being the shortest route, had only two stages. Prior to the introduction of this new equipment, passengers paid 3d to ride inside the tram and 2d to ride outside. By good fortune, one of these fare collection boxes survives in a local museum.

Bolton Corporation introduced the Bell Punch system on its trams, and an advert depicting one of these punches is shown on page 79. For use with this punch, conductors were issued with a wooden rack which held, under a spring clip, pre-printed coloured tickets for the various fare values. Initially the tickets were of the geographic type, but all the examples shown opposite were of the numeric type, which succeeded the original type. The conductor punched a hole in the ticket against the stage number (name in the case of the original tickets) where the passenger had boarded, and the ticket value represented how far the passenger could travel. The punched clippings were retained inside the machine and could be checked for administrative purposes against the register which was incorporated on the punch. As the conductor punched the ticket, a loud audible ring could be heard, which discouraged the fraudulent re-use of tickets. The reverse of the ticket was most often used for advertising purposes, a useful source of income for the department. Even the firms using this advertising medium, hidden on the reverse, make interesting reading today.

The Bell Punch system was replaced by the TIM system in Bolton in 1940, initially on the trams. Again an example of a TIM machine is shown on page 79 and this system was considered a significant step forward as it utilised blank rolls of paper, on to which the appropriate information, including the fare, would be printed. The actual ticket was issued by a quick turn of a handle provided for the purpose. At a stroke this system reduced significantly the amount of ticket stocks required and, correspondingly, the number of administrative staff required to manage the system. The major feature of the TIM machine was its telephone-like dial, which permitted the conductor to pre-set the ticket value by 'dialling' the appropriate amount.

In due course the TIM machine was replaced by the Setright Speed model. Working on the same basis as the TIM and utilising blank rolls, the Setright had separate dials for shillings and pence and was therefore more flexible than its predecessor, particularly when fares were being increased at fairly regular intervals.

Opposite is a selection of tickets, all of which date from the pre-decimalisation period, decimalisation occurring in February 1971. For those under 40 years old it should perhaps be explained that the pre-decimalisation pound consisted of twenty shillings each divided into twelve pence, the old pound therefore having 240 pence rather than 100. Prices were normally written as £14 12s 8d, single pence values being shown as merely 3d. The tickets shown opposite are described using their unique number.

D44 8467 This ½d ticket was the minimum value ticket ever used and this particular example has been overprinted for use in connection with children's fares.

N33 8859 To ticket enthusiasts' apparently this type of ticket is known as a 'Grandfather Clock' style and is for 2½d.

U108 6496 is another 2½d ticket, but this time for use on shorter routes as only 17 stages have been accommodated on the ticket.

P18 5167 This 4d one only has provision for 15 stages in the more simplified style.

Y 5637 Another overprinted ticket, this time for a child's 9d return. Instead of stage numbers it carries the numeric days of the month on its face and was also only for use on what Bolton Corporation described as a 'Co-ordinated Motor Bus Service' (ie a jointly operated route).

O1 0537 This adult return ticket not only carries the days of the month on it, but also the moths themselves. Return tickets would have had a limited period of validity. It also carries the legend 'Bolton Corporation Omnibuses', a title only in use for a limited period and for good measure is overprinted 'BCO'.

Y29 5878 Workman's fares were a significant feature of bus and tram operation during the 20th century and were often enshrined in the enabling Acts of Parliament. This 3d return has provision for indicating the day of issue (workman's return were usually day returns), although on this example the hole has been punched neatly between Wednesday and Thursday (!), and also for the hour of return, which has not been punched. Perhaps this worker didn't return home that day. In the event that there was any doubt about the validity of the ticket, it has also been overprinted with a large 'W'.

V43 7548 The narrative of this book has made frequent reference to the considerable involvement of the Corporation with the South Lancashire Transport Company This 2d ticket is not only endorsed 'Joint Ticket' but carries both the operators' names for use on such services.

Cx 4301 Bolton Corporation sold pre-paid books of ten tickets as illustrated here.

9325 The TIM system utilised blank paper rolls onto which the machine would print the necessary detail. This 3d ticket was issued on 22nd June 1962.

O866 The Setright system used similar principles to TIM, with almost blank rolls having the journey information printed by the machine. The Setright system allowed a greater range of fare values as this one shilling ticket demonstrates.

Bolton Buses in Colour

A selection of photographs taken by Geoff Lumb showing the original maroon bus livery, with the three cream bands, the Plymouth red and cream, and the later cherry liveries through to the maroon and off-white of the Atlantean era.

The two double-deckers in the upper left illustration are standing outside the home of the late Fred Dibnah, whilst in the lower left illustration the now-preserved single-decker Crossley DBN 978 can be seen in its Welfare Department livery outside Shiffnall Street Garage. *(GL all)*

Preserved Bolton Vehicles in Colour
– a small selection

Daddy of them all has to be tramcar 66, built in 1901/02, withdrawn from service in 1946, rescued for preservation in 1963 and put back into service – in Blackpool, since Bolton no longer had any tram lines – in 1981. Only the lower deck had survived and it was restored, complete with 'new' bogies and all electrics, and fully-painted, lettered and lined as seen here. Proudly standing on the platform is Derek Shepherd, the man behind this and many other tramcar rebuilding schemes. Derek's enthusiasm for Bolton and all things to do with trams has been channelled into the appropriate sections of this book, for which we thank him.

Below we see 66 on just another outing in Blackpool – after more than 25 years there perhaps they should give it the Freedom of the Borough?
(DS collection; HP)

Bolton's pre-war policy of withdrawing its buses after a relatively short life meant there was often still plenty of life left in them. This Titan TD1 was sold for further service and, eventually, rescued for preservation, passing back into its original maker's ownership. As part of Leyland's heritage collection it was rebuilt back to open staircase configuration as seen here at an open day at RAF Waddington, where it was operating a Park-and Ride service. It is now part of the LVVS collection in Lincoln. The Crossley-bodied single-decker Crossley, seen below, owes its survival to use in the Welfare fleet (as seen on page 155), after withdrawal. It was caught on camera with its fellow, the Orion-bodied Bolton PD2, in Manchester's Heaton Park at a Trans-Pennine event, always a good opportunity to see preserved buses in pleasant surroundings. *(JAS both)*

Manchester's Museum of Transport in Boyle Street, Cheetham Hill, is another good place to see preserved Bolton buses. The resident Orion PD2 number 77 is seen opposite, with Atlantean number 232 in the photograph alongside. On this page two styles of Atlanteans can be compared, 232 above and 6809 (309) below; the latter was delivered to SELNEC but is seen here as preserved in the GMT livery which had been changed to a darker shade of orange and a paler shade of white – did someone like pop music in those days? The lower view, like that overleaf, was taken at one of the splendid *Heart of the Pennines* rallies, this being the 1994 event. *(JAS both)*